Aesthetics Ho!

Essays on art, literature, and theatre

D. Sidney-Fryer has written or edited the following books:

Poems in Prose, by Clark Ashton Smith (1965)
Etchings in Ivory, poems in prose by Robert E. Howard (1968)
Other Dimensions, short stories by Clark Ashton Smith (1970)
Songs and Sonnets Atlantean: The First Series (1971)
Selected Poems, omnibus by Clark Ashton Smith (1971)
The Last of the Great Romantic Poets, i.e., Clark Ashton Smith (1973)
Emperor of Dreams: A Clark Ashton Smith Bibliography (1978)
The Black Book of Clark Ashton Smith, his commonplace book (1979)
A Vision of Doom, poems by Ambrose Bierce (1980)
The Case of the Light Fantastic Toe: The Romantic Ballet and Signor Maestro Cesare Pugni—A Chronicle and Source Book (magnum opus, unpublished MS. produced 1980–2000
The City of the Singing Flame, tales by Clark Ashton Smith (1981)
The Last Incantation, tales by Clark Ashton Smith (1982)
The Monster of the Prophecy, tales by Clark Ashton Smith (1983)
Strange Shadows: The Uncollected Fiction and Essays of Clark Ashton Smith, edited by Steve Behrends with Donald Sidney-Fryer and Rah Hoffman (1989)
The Hashish-Eater; or, The Apocalypse of Evil, 1922 version, by Clark Ashton Smith (1990; with CD 2008 performed by D. Sidney-Fryer)
As Green as Emeraude: The Collected Poems of Margo Skinner (1990)
The Devil's Notebook (complete epigrams and apothegms) by Clark Ashton Smith, edited with Don Herron (1990)
Songs and Sonnets Atlantean: The Second Series (2003)
Gaspard de la Nuit, by Aloysius Bertrand, translation (2004)
Songs and Sonnets Atlantean: The Third Series (2005)
The Atlantis Fragments: The trilogy of "Songs and Sonnets Atlantean," omnibus (2008, 2009)
The Outer Gate: The Collected Poems of Nora May French (2009)
The Golden State Phastasticks: The California Romantics and Related Subjects: Collected Essays and Reviews, edited with Leo Grin and Alan Gullette (2011)
The Atlantis Fragments, The Novel: The Existing Chronicle: A Vision of the Final Days (2011)
Hobgoblin Apollo: The Autobiography of Donald Sidney-Fryer (2016)
Odds & Ends (poetry, 2016)
The Averoigne Chronicles, by Clark Ashton Smith, edited by Ron Hilger with Donald Sidney-Fryer (2016)
West of Wherevermore and Other Travel Writings (2016)
Aesthetics Ho! Essays on art, literature, and theatre (2017)
Ends and Odds (poetry, 2017)

AESTHETICS HO!

ESSAYS ON ART, LITERATURE, AND THEATRE

―――

TOGETHER WITH RELATED SUBJECTS

Donald Sidney-Fryer

Hippocampus Press
―――
New York

Aesthetics Ho! and *Ends and Odds* copyright © 2017 by Hippocampus Press.

Works by Donald Sidney-Fryer copyright © 2017 Donald Sidney-Fryer.

Grateful acknowledgement is made to G. Sutton Breiding for permission to reprint his poem "San Francisco," © 1975 by Sutton Breiding for the Fugitive Press. Ditto to D. Sidney-Fryer for his poem "Atlantis," copyright © 1971 by Sidney-Fryer for Arkham House, on behalf of the First Series of *Songs and Sonnets Atlantean*. Review by Mark Purcell on pp. 117–18 is reproduced from *Nyctalops* by permission of the publisher, Harry O. Morris.

The cover artwork, "Prelude to an Orgy" by Hannes Bok, is also known as "Prelude to the Afternoon of a Faun." Commissioned by Rah Hoffman in the 1940s directly from the artist, it is said to be the only Bok watercolor in existence. Thanks are due to Ron Hilger, with whom the original resides, and Jerad Walters of Centipede Press, who kindly provided the image. Cover design by Kevin I. Slaughter.

All rights reserved. Except for review purposes, no part of this book may be reproduced or transmitted in any form or by any means, electronic or mechanical, including photocopying, recording or by any information storage and retrieval system, without permission in writing from the publisher.

Published by Hippocampus Press
P.O. Box 641, New York, NY 10156
www.hippocampuspress.com

Cover artwork by Hannes Bok.

Hippocampus Press logo designed by Anastasia Damianakos.

First Edition
1 3 5 7 9 8 6 4 2

ISBN 978-1-61498-201-2

DEDICATED
TO JOHN-CHARLES MORAN

*otherwise Juan-Carlos Morán,
"The Romantist" for our times,
in memoriam.*

Contents

Aesthetics Ho! 9
    Introduction 11
    Jesse Allen's First Mural 15
    A Defense and Illustration of One Poetic Method 27
    San Francisco, by G. Sutton Breiding 51
    A Note on History and/or Historiography 53
    Old versus New 58
    Poetry and Poetry Again 63
    Perfect Form, Perfect Shape 78
    Atlantis 84
    One Poetic Practice 85
    H. P. Lovecraft—A Belated Homage 94
    Flickering Shadows on a Lighted Screen 99
    Intangibility 104
    That's Hollywood? That's Hollywood! 107
    Farewell to All That 111
    Appendix 115
Ends and Odds 119

Aesthetics Ho!
Essays on art, literature, and theatre

Introduction

Let me declare my purpose at once in writing the present monograph, since everyone these days appears to have serious intentions, whether political or non-political, of declaring a given stance transparently and forthrightly, as if such has never happened before in history.

Despite the title this book is not a disquisition (or inquisition) on aesthetics in general. It is only an account of my direct encounter with the subject as exemplified in various individuals, most of them artists of various types and in varying degrees.

Early in the 1960s, when I was living and working in Auburn outside Sacramento on an off-and-on-again basis—I did not move to Northern California until 1965—I became acquainted with a once close friend of the poet and fictioneer Clark Ashton Smith (also known as C. Ashton Smith à la A. Conan Doyle). This person was Genevieve K. Sully, to whom Ashton Smith dedicated an entire cycle of love poems, *The Jasmine Girdle,* as well as his first major prose collection, *Out of Space and Time* (1942). At one time in her house we were discussing poetry traditional and non-traditional, beautiful and unbeautiful, meaningful and non-meaningful—that is, according to our own perceptions and preferences.

We happened to share much in common, and we realized that at once—a source of comfort for both of us. We did not need to waste valuable time in finding common ground. On the spur of the moment I recited (from memory) the last verse paragraph (the last 26 lines) from that magical and not overlong narrative in sonorous verse, "Duandon," from *The House of Orchids* (1911) by the poet George Sterling, Ashton Smith's great friend and mentor from 1911 until Sterling's death in late 1926.

Genevieve responded favorably at once to my resonant, full-voiced, and rhythmical recital of these last lines, and kindly noted that Smith would certainly have approved of my recitation style, just as she did herself. That made me conscious that aesthetically we happened to find ourselves on the exact same page (no pun intended), yet all the more.

The lady of *The Jasmine Girdle* surely was no stranger to Sterling's poetry, since her lifetime had encompassed his *floruit* in San Francisco and the Monterey area, no less than on the Californian West Coast in general. Encouraged even more by her approbation, I pointedly mentioned this aesthetic certitude between us, not something that I could share with just anyone, but that I could share with her.

A portentous pause, and then with little further ado she declared with utter sincerity, speaking for that pre-hippie period, "Donald, aesthetics in our time are dead." So unexpectedly did Genevieve pronounce this, with such vehemence, with such solemnity, that it surprised and startled me beyond measure. It was as if she had uttered a moral judgment in biblical terms. And in a certain sense she was not mistaken.

But we must not be too narrow in our perception of aesthetics, which one of my dictionaries usefully defines as that branch of philosophy dealing with the nature of beauty, of art, and of taste, the last an often unknown quantity or "element." Aesthetics above all also deals with the creation and appreciation of the beautiful, of the fine and the applied arts.

Genevieve's own set of aesthetics reflected those of her own earlier time-frame, that is, formed by those living before World War I. In the late 1800s and early 1900s a veritable Cult of Beauty (if not Religion) existed among the aesthetes internationally, both creative people and critics, including the French Parnassians, the French Symbolists, as well as the British Symbolists.

This movement also exerted a strong influence among artists and writers in the United States, whether East Coast, West Coast, or the Midwest, including our own California Romantics, Bierce, Sterling, Ashton Smith, Nora May French, and so forth. Overall it proved a vital and beneficial influence, preserving much of the country from an artless provincialism.

Purely by chance Genevieve's aesthetics happened to coincide with my own, but I had formed or formulated mine independently of hers and her earlier life. Many influences had gone into shaping my own aesthetics, not only the art direction in the feature films of the 1930s and 1940s, but especially my college classical preparatory courses in language and literature in high school.

Later, largely during the 1950s, Ashton Smith with his fiction and above all his poetry, and then even later, during the 1960s, Edmund Spenser with *The Faerie Queene* and *The Shepheardes Calender,* greatly reinforced and refined my own set or sense of aesthetics. It is then in that older sense that I invoke the philosophy of the beautiful in this introduction and in this volume, however odd or unfashionable that might seem today.

And it is in that older sense that I try to bring aesthetics back to life, thus a piece of necromancy, or as it were in the present case, a piece of white magick.

When in a period of doubt and shifting values in art or life—faced with what may seem a barren and intractable present—the creative individual, searching for some creative gambit or premise that he can ride on into the future, can yet always turn to the recent or the distant past, in order that he may find notable and solid examples that will prove of greater use and inspiration to him than from his immediate contemporaries.

Or the artist can also turn, at the same time and just as readily, back to his own and native roots as both a person and a creative individual. This is not a new predicament for creative people, but has occurred throughout history. I take an example from among my close friends. When the Kenyan and *echt*-African artist Jesse Allen began seriously to paint as an adolescent and then as a young adult, he faced the same dilemma. As he began to look around him at the then art scene—this was during the 1950s and the 1960s—what should he see but the advanced evolution of Abstract Expressionism in the mid-twentieth century! This movement emphasized the painter's freedom to suggest attitudes and emotions via non-traditional and usually non-representational means.

Riding this wave more or less in triumph as they were (after their own hard, long struggle to gain recognition and to reach their own artistic peak), Jesse examined such artists as Jackson Pollock, Mark Rothko, and other painters. Given his own Muse and inner vision, what could Jesse find among their typical canvases to serve him as guide or inspiration? Nothing, or very little. He had to look deep into himself, but he had already discovered his typical imagery—Africa perceived through the prism of his artistic imagination. The promised land lay within himself. He but needed to continue what he began in his mid-adolescence, already a highly original mode or style of envisioning and painting.

Thus I myself as a poet faced a situation almost the same as the one confronted by Jesse as an artist-painter, but no less difficult, if not more awkward, at more or less about the same time. But as compared to him and his dilemma, I came personally to my vocation somewhat later than he did. I had attained my middle twenties when I began seriously to create my own and characteristic poetry.

Whereas dear Jesse, valiant artist that he remains to this day, faced that intimidating dragon called Abstract Expressionism, I faced a confused and perplexing mishmash of poetry traditional and non-traditional, not helped significantly by that arbiter elegantiae in matters poetical, the then poetry editor first of the *Saturday Review of Literature* and then later of the *Saturday Review,* to wit, John Ciardi. I had grown up with his pontifical pronouncements (or as they thus appeared to me learning and evolving in high school at that time), that is, during the late 1940s and early 1950s.

But then the California Romantics, headed by Ashton Smith and Ambrose Bierce, came to my rescue, not that I could imitate them. However, I did pointedly notice Bierce's indifference to the ordinary or conventional concerns of humanity, but more strategically Ashton Smith's cosmic-astronomic-mindedness. As I pondered the implications of the latter, his originality became rather more apparent and hit me in the face with its full implications as applied to conventional religion and conventional pieties.

In discovering and assimilating Spenser, I returned to the source that had inspired not only his Elizabethan contemporaries but any number of other poets big and small from the time of his own *floruit* on into our own period, including many conspicuous figures who superficially could not seem less like him and his own multifaceted work!

In the following essays I make many general statements, unavoidable as it turns out, and in spite of their tone I do not intend any of them to be dogmatic in any way. In the course of this monograph I touch upon many subjects as connected to the arts of whatever type, and by that very choice I purposely avoid anything that deals with politics (as nebulous a subject as poetics!), except as it relates to still vibrant issues of artistic expression and creation.

—Donald Sidney-Fryer

Auburn, California,
7 February 2017.

Jesse Allen's First Mural

Today is Saturday (possibly still sacred to Saturn), 17 December 2016. The three of us, painter-artist Jesse Allen, his irreplaceable assistant (and chief enabler of almost everything) Eric Marenco, and I, writer-poet Donald Sidney-Fryer, arrived in San Salvador on Tuesday morning, 29 November, via a red-eye flight on Avianca Airlines from San Francisco Airport. After a few days and nights of rest, we had all recovered from the fatigue of the physical transition from Northern California to El Salvador, especially as felt by Jesse and myself in our early eighties, meaning the lack of sleep in a regular bed in a dark and quiet bedroom.

As creative people, Jesse and I derive much of our ongoing balance (psychic, emotional, spiritual) from our creativity on a continual basis. In pursuance of that, I have already written my first short poems here. More importantly, since I derive some general inspiration from his art, his now many paintings, I must report that Jesse began on or around Wednesday, 7 December, to sketch with his special graphite pencil his very first mural anywhere at all on the walls of the big main room in the main house or building here.

A word or two as to the where that is here: the hacienda, or multicrop farm (as distinct from a finca, or one-crop farm), including coffee, fruits, maize, and other vegetables. The hacienda now functions under the name of Jalenco, a word combined from Jesse Allen and Eric Marenco, obviously *jal* and *enco.* About an hour or more west of the capital San Salvador by regular motor vehicle, the property lies just west of Candelaria de la Frontera (itself only fifteen or twenty minutes away by vehicle), the frontier or border shared with Guatemala. I shall describe the hacienda (twenty-two acres or so) and the compound (some seven separate structures) later as I continue writing this essay. One important interior detail: the maximum height in the main house, floor to ceiling, measures about twenty feet, and the average height otherwise in the rest of the house about twelve feet or so.

The mural begins about four feet from the floor and extends upward some six or eight feet (the height varies), the walls being originally painted with an off-white or ivory, in this way making a good surface for Jesse to paint with his (water-based) acrylics, his preferred medium, far less complicated than oils with their array of turpentines and other thinners. By creating his first mural indoors, he need not fret about a sudden heavy rain messing up his designs and colors, as he would outdoors, that is, unless protected by an overhead covering. As launched so far on seven different walls, Jesse will also do a separate marine tableau on the one main wall in the bedroom just off the kitchen or dining area, the bedchamber that Jesse and I share with separate beds.

For any connoisseur familiar with Jesse's characteristic imagery as revealed in his now many paintings, it comes as a pleasant surprise, if not indeed as an almost startling revelation, to perceive and recognize that same imagery, but now done on a much larger scale, that is, as writ large. To date, off and on, he has used the skills of a young and quite gifted artist, one Alberto (or "Beto") Tovar-Merino, a natural talent if there ever was one, to help him to fill in the colors in much of the overall panorama. So far, so good, the mural makes a brave show!

Not very far from the main gate, the compound contains seven structures, most of them completed. First, the garage, and next to it (not yet built), an overstructure, the guest house, above the extra vehicle-parking spaces. Walkways envelop most of the other buildings and lead in and out of the various courtyards. Leaving the garage, we enter at once Jesse's future studio, a kind of suite: one huge and high chamber with a special partition to demarcate his actual quarters on the eastern side. At the south end of the studio, a bathroom with shower, toilet, and wash basin (nothing yet installed). Very high ceiling. Plenty of natural daylight coming in through the window spaces, the windows not yet installed. A courtyard comes next and adjoins the main house, which in turn adjoins a larger courtyard further on.

A carpenter presently uses the studio to help in the further construction wherever needed on the property. He also makes furniture. In one-half of this indoor space (the half that Jesse will occupy) someone has neatly piled up quite a bit of lumber, including big planks, mostly local woods. As an artist's very own specially designed atelier it will make a superb studio.

Facing west, the main and only door—a double-paneled entrance, much of it beautifully hand-carved—leads directly into the main chamber, or salon, of the main house. This is a combined living room and eating space with a twenty-foot ceiling at its highest, but not an uniform height. This area flows at once on into the big kitchen. Minus the kitchen, these are the walls upon which Jesse is now sketching and painting his first mural, thus protected from the rain and other elements. The two bathrooms and the two bedrooms with closet alcoves complete the roster of the chambers in the main house, with three handmade bedsteads created by Gonzalo, the carpenter using the studio.

We continue south across the courtyard from the main house, to enter a large storage edifice (with washer and dryer), standing in the southeast corner of the compound, and east of the courtyard adjoining the smaller (arcaded brick) house of the young caretaker couple, José and Lupita Hernandez, with little daughter Adela. Passing by the big river gate that opens onto the river road (it sits up high), we continue west to the large two-part chicken coop. Just north of that, the all-essential water tower stands, supported by four square corner columns, with water tank at the top, and at the bottom a square walled-in (open) tank, a kind of miniature swimming pool. Just northeast of the water tower we come to the solid stone fenced-in doghouse for the six thin, medium-sized canines, three males and three females. They wander around on the property, but hang out in and around the compound. This completes the roster of the structures on the property inside the compound walls.

Passing through the river gate and at once across the river road, we descend some thirty feet or so to the extensive riverbank area, still about six feet above the actual stream itself running north and south, just a mere trickle now. Trees and their shade dominate this level space next to the river, distinguished by six or seven giant ceiba trees, as well as by smaller ones, one of the giants rising close to the others but just across the stream. Another giant, the most massive, must be hundreds of years old. Its immense trunk and buttress-roots make it a thing of wonder and awe. Unlike the giant redwoods or some species of pine trees, the ceibas in maturity often look very different from one another. This grove remains a very special place, if not sacred, to Eric, Jesse, and myself.

I have reconnoitered up and down our little river, and have discovered that other giant ceibas exist, just as remarkable in and of themselves as our own trees. What then makes our grove stand out? The fact that the trees making it up are all easily accessible along one continuous and level space, with plenty of natural seats where one may sit and contemplate slightly varying vistas.

Today is Monday, 19 December 2016, and I continue to write this quasi-diary account of Jesse Allen's first mural as done on the main interior walls of the main house. Sunday went by quietly for just about everyone as a day of rest. I should mention that, born in 1936, Jesse has been drawing and painting since childhood and professionally since 1966, when Muldoon Elder, the owner of the then brand-new Vorpal Gallery, agreed to feature Jesse and his art along with other artists. Muldoon maintained the gallery at that time at its first location, on the Embarcadero in San Francisco. Since then, Jesse has had many exhibits, whether via the Vorpal Gallery (at its successive and sometimes multiple locations) or via other galleries in other cities, including New York. Jesse works at his painting (in this case, the mural) every day, alternating periods of intense concentration and action with periods of repose flat on his back in bed.

Jesse figures that he has now completed about one-half or two-thirds of the mural, with another two weeks to go (probably an underestimate), perhaps finishing it (for the most part) around New Year's Day. As an artist working on a smaller scale, he usually fills *in* the painting, but here within the terms dictated by the interior walls, no less than the scale commensurate with a mural, he is filling it all *out*, so as to speak.

Today, rather than Alberto, another but much older and more experienced painter, Lerey (pronounced lay-RAY), is helping Jesse and to a considerable extent filling *in* more or less as Jesse himself might do. Lerey, a small, trim, still handsome older man, has both amiability and a certain *gravitas,* quite enjoyable overall, as are so many of the people in this country, a great benefit for anyone residing here, especially a stranger like myself. I hope that we shall indeed have Alberto with us again, besides his being one of our housekeeper Miriam's very own children. Otherwise he works as a waiter (he has great social skills) as his main job.

Tuesday, 20 December 2016. Lerey overnighted in a sleeping bag on the beautiful tile floor of the storage building. With Jesse, he continues to work on the mural, which now has a bottom strip realized in standard acrylic yellow. Lerey has now filled in much of the panorama, thus freeing Jesse to concentrate on other and more creative details. Lerey is seventy and thus ten years or so younger than Jesse and myself, and makes a simpático companion. Like many artists, he remains a cultured and cultivated individual. Alberto showed up again today and continues to fill in the mural here and there. Thus at this point of conception, evolution, and execution we leave the multi-paneled panorama that the mural has become. Lerey has begun a mural-size copy of *Gallus*—the *Gallo,* or *Rooster*—on the one big panel of the inner compound wall between the studio and the main house.

Wednesday, 21 December 2016. Lerey overnighted again in the storage building and continues to copy the earlier painting. Alberto is also on hand and continues to fill in the panorama under Jesse's direction. Today marks a full two weeks since Jesse began the mural, and although not complete, it certainly looks like it, or something very close. The titular chanticleer of *Gallus,* one of Jesse's best fantasticated critters, shows up well against the yellow background as in the original painting. *Panorama de mural, adiós hasta más tarde, mañana.*

I have just discovered, concerning the picture with frame next to the kitchen in the main room (three feet high by one and a half feet wide, made or sculpted out of the same piece of Salvadoran wood), showing a volcano above and a magnificent bull below, that Lerey created this himself. Thus he is both a complete sculptor (at least in wood) and a complete painter, hence an all-around accomplished artist. A fine person, great company, and although he takes pride in his work of whatever type (as any self-respecting artist would), he is as free from ego, everyday or artistic, as ever I have encountered.

The astute reader might well ask and wonder why no big fancy art book has yet appeared on Jesse and his paintings, especially since he first became well or better known thanks to the article on him and his art (with the painting "Two Macaques" reproduced on the issue's cover) that appeared in the spring or summer of 1968 in the Sunday Magazine section of the combined *San Francisco Chronicle* and *Examiner.* This article alerted many people, including me, to Jesse's existence and his unique style of painting. His art appealed, and still appeals, to myself in a manner that no other art ever has. In subsequent years various close friends and aficionados all donated to what became a large sum of money to produce such a book. A close friend of Jesse's, Norman Bryson (from England, but whom he met in San Francisco), wrote a brilliant and insightful text to accompany the paintings, exceptionally well chosen to demonstrate the artist's depth and range. Unfortunately, these efforts came to nothing, the money became pre-empted for something else. Although temporarily shelved, the art book project remains alive and might yet bring forth something remarkable.

Jesse and his paintings have generally received an excellent response from the public itself wherever exhibited in the U.S., including San Francisco and Manhattan; and a mixed range of reaction from the critics, more often indifferent than negative. As I witnessed it at the time (living in San Francisco during 1965-75), I recall how the then two major art critics (writing for the then two leading daily newspapers) responded to Jesse's earliest exhibits at the Vorpal Gallery. After a long life and career pontificating on the arts in their various manifestations, the well-fleshed and self-satisfied Alfred Frankenstein (Dr. Frankenstein, indeed!) once mentioned Jesse in passing as one of the "mediocre artists" featured at the Vorpal; this occurred in the *Examiner.* The much younger Thomas Albright, who wrote for the *Chronicle,* evidently baffled by certain aspects of Jesse's paintings, could only characterize his work overall as "trance art," inasmuch as it attracted the connoisseur-critic but without allowing him to draw any further conclusions, and that it existed in a realm beyond facile interpretation, or explanation, at least as practiced by museums, professional critics, etc. By an odd coincidence Frankenstein himself did not live that much longer, and the unfortunate Albright, who suffered from ill health much of his life, died sometime after that.

In addition to the caretaker couple here—Lupita looks after both houses in terms of the kitchen, cleaning, and cooking, and José looks after many things in the compound and on the property (the overall twenty-two acres)—we have the services of an excellent housekeeper, Miriam Tovar-Merino, usually accompanied by Fatima, her eleven-year-old daughter, her new six-month-old son Mateu, and often her adult artist son Alberto, or "Beto," who has been helping Jesse quite a bit with selected aspects of the panorama-mural. Miriam does most of the cleaning in the main house, but above all she works in the kitchen, preparing most of the meals as well as many foods in advance of inclusion in a meal. But everyone pitches in a little with the cleaning and food preparation as we go from day to day. Sometimes a few extra people work in the compound, and Miriam feeds them as well (usually the midday meal that here takes place in the early afternoon). Thus, thanks to a handful of people, all assiduous workers, the household functions very well on a practical basis.

Xmas Day (X, the unknown quantity?), truly a day of rest for everyone, at least in the main house. Jesse and I took a nap in the late morning (it is now the early afternoon). I'm writing at the moment, Eric Sr. naps on the big bed in his bedroom suite, Eric Jr. sleeps in one of the two outdoor hammocks, and Jesse now sleeps in the other. Both hammocks hang in an extensive roofed-over part of the courtyard between the main house and the caretaker couple's cottage. So, the house of the sleeping beauties, indeed! Eric Sr. just now got up and is making some scrumptious turkey sandwiches for all four of us, and the others have just arisen as well.

As ever, Jesse continues to work on selected aspects or details in the mural. (The usual household workers have both Saturday and Sunday—that is, the entire Xmas weekend—off, and we wait on ourselves.) Between the elephant couple, mother and father (the extreme left-hand side of the panorama) Jesse has today painted in a baby elephant as cute as can be, that is, cute within the terms of Jesse's often fantasticated African critters. Overall Jesse is currently bringing out in more vivid form some of the half-dozen animals or so dispersed throughout the panels or walls that make up the panorama-mural.

The local people who have viewed and studied the mural react in an enlightened manner to it. Even if Central America has its own jungles, mountains, and feral creatures, they know right off that what they are regarding reflects Africa, and not the tropical Americas. Despite or because of his developed sense of fantasy, they sense and identify the African genesis at once.

Friday, 30 December 2016. The weather has remained fresh and comfortable, the range of temperature c. 85° to 65°—sometimes a little higher or a little lower. After working here this last period of the workweek since Monday, 26 December, and moreover working very long and very hard each and every day, at least eight hours or more, the *pintor-mago* (painter-magus) Lerey has gone home not just for Sunday, 1 January 2017, but for the entire weekend. Most people in El Salvador work six days a week, Monday through Saturday, but Xmas and New Year's remain special, and many people have the entire weekend to use as they wish. Most of those who do not work this Saturday and Sunday spend it at home with their families.

Lerey well deserves a major rest. From Jesse he has taken over the task of putting much of the reiterative detail into the mural's assortment of scattered rocks and varied plant life, whether palm trees or other kinds, ground-hugging plants with lavish leaves, and so forth. This filling-in of reiterative detail constitutes hard work indeed, and has lightened Jesse's own labor considerably. It has also permitted him the periods of rest that he needs at eighty or eighty-one, not to mention his many pills! Even if his painting is keeping him alive, it can also markedly fatigue him, and so these brief moments of repose help him recover beyond measure. Lerey also well deserves whatever fee Eric pays him. The bossman here, Eric, has just left with Lerey, along with housekeeper Miriam and her family. Eric is driving them all home in Santa Ana. We shall probably not see Eric again until early evening after dark, which comes after 5:30 P.M. It is dark by six.

Our other housekeeper Lupe, or Lupita, takes care of our evening meals and related services. She and her husband José both look after the property and its buildings, meaning above all the others those in the compound. Eric makes sure that Jesse, Eric, and I receive more than adequate attention. I must confess, however, that I prefer to look after myself and my living space. The idea of being attended is foreign to me.

And so, where do we find ourselves relative to the panorama-mural? A full three weeks have now passed since Jesse began the mural by sketching the shapes and patterns of his imagery with his charcoal pencils. Soon after that the coloring also began, thus almost at once, with Alberto helping Jesse. A week or so following that, thanks to Eric, Lerey as a very skilled and experienced (professional) painter arrived on the scene to help Jesse still more. As the result of three painters working almost side by side, the mural finds itself about eighty percent complete, with another week to go before finalization. As a vast and unique painting it will make the main house and the overall property celebrated, and properly so. We shall return to the subject of the mural on New Year's Day.

Sunday, 1 January 2017. As on last weekend, and as on last Sunday, distinguished by fireworks animated by caretaker José, we had once again some similar and even more abundant explosions, from big (very loud like bullet shots) to middling to small (but all of them loud), starting in the very late afternoon (say, 5 P.M.) and ending finally sometime before 10 P.M. Except as a special display prepared by professionals, fireworks per se have never appealed to me nor to Jesse, neither the visual nor the aural. When they finished, we could finally lapse into sleep, albeit we had gone to bed in the darkness before 7 P.M. The one great thing about the fireworks is that it silences the six skinny dogs with their often incessant barking, above all at night, and sends them far from the compound and out of our hearing. Their sensitive ears, never mind ours, cannot abide the sound of the fireworks, the loudest about as loud as guns or pistols going off.

Even without holiday celebration, several well-timed firecrackers early at night or early in the morning (but after everyone awakes) help keep the baying of the hounds in check, particularly in the middle of the night. About a week ago, everyone in the compound passed a terrible night almost without sleep. The dogs barked very loudly, almost constantly, but they had cause enough. A group of local men were hunting down in and around the terrain occupied by our grove of ceiba trees.

At long last Eric as the boss got up out of bed and went outside and then down to the river, where he discovered, and met, the local hunters who were keeping our dogs barking and on the alert. He asked the hunters to leave and threatened them with the police in case they should return. Thus went the night of the hunters—*así transcurrió la noche de la cazadores*—nor have they returned.

Even when the artist of whatever type (painting, literature, music, and so forth) arranges his time and space for maximum efficiency in terms of creative expression, that does not guarantee it will turn out that way. The practical concerns of everyday living often interfere or dictate otherwise. In our own situation the lack of one good night's rest did not spell disaster so much as it did much greater fatigue than usual. We slept very well the next night! Like many older people, Jesse and I do not always rest soundly during the long night hours, and so a few naps during the even longer day will make up for the lost nocturnal sleep.

Wednesday, 4 January 2016. Lerey, that valiant little man, did not reappear on Monday, but had to go to a hospital, not to remain there but to consult with a doctor. Off and on he has had problems with his lungs (like Jesse, he once smoked cigarettes), but whatever problem emerged, his condition has improved, and he returned to the hacienda today. Delighted and reassured to have him with us again, we all greeted him with extra warmth. He no longer works on the mural exclusively, but somewhere else in the compound, pursuing his art of sculpture in wood, by making more furniture, as always elegant and simple. Among other pieces he is carving medallions for the big iron entrance gate, and a big fancy bed for Jesse's use in the studio, where I, too, shall have my own bed and quarters (much simpler and smaller), all on the same side (the eastern) of the high, large studio building.

This weekend should see the mural-panorama completed, or almost thus, even if Jesse continues to fuss with it, a remarkable and impressive achievement. Soon shall Jesse collaborate with Lerey on a series of large canvases, the inner and outer frames to be made on the property, but the canvas materials must come from the U.S. to assure a better quality than what is for sale in the capital. Without Lerey the straightforward and rapid production of new paintings could not happen, something to ponder. Eric seems to have in mind a kind of mass production but not assembly-line. A genuine factory-style process would not turn out to be either possible or desirable, at least for buyers paying top dollar for artistic integrity or authenticity.

Finishing up the mural is taking longer than what Jesse has estimated from time to time, as if a month or a little more does not represent an incredibly brief time in which to achieve a panorama stretching across seven walls! Meanwhile, for my own reasons I must return to Northern California, not only for ongoing medical reasons but to secure myself a new residence in Sacramento. Eric must also return, but for business reasons. He has just changed our tickets (Avianca Airlines) so we can both go back at the same time, Sunday, 22 January, involving a considerable fee for the change in date. Such does not come cheap!

Wednesday, 18 January 2017. Two weeks later. Immense progress on the mural! The young assistant Alberto has literally dropped out of the picture due to external circumstances. The mural is essentially finished, even if Jesse and Lerey continue to fuss with certain details here and there. The completed product has turned out as promised by its genesis and earlier development. An impressive accomplishment by any and all standards, duly described and praised by me in the given context. I lay down my pen after I pen this, amen.

Afterword

I must add here as a kind of postscript some kind of a brief, general description of the panorama-mural with its seven walls or panels. It begins on the left or north of the main door. It goes from left to right (or west, north, east, and south) and measures about forty-five feet in length. It starts about four feet from the floor and extends upward variously from six to eight to ten feet.

Individual feet after the panel numbers pertain to length of the panels. Differently colored "washes" (largely green and blue, with some purple and yellow) indicate the heavens in all the panels, which also feature all manner of birds, plants, rocks, planets, trees of two main types (palms and regular branched trees), and so forth, all part of Jesse's characteristic imagery.

Panels 1 & 2 (5 ft. & 6 ft.): Regular branched tree with blue trunk right in the corner (straddling it) linking both panels. Mother elephant with cute baby pachyderm in front of her on left panel. Father elephant on right panel.

Panel 3 (12 ft.): Palm tree, Brahma-like bull, regular branched tree with blue trunk, tortoise, large plant with large luxuriant leaves, tortoise, goat (straddling the corner between panels 3 & 4), big sickle moon above (between) large-leaved plant and cute little goat.

Panel 4 (5 ft.): Mostly the heavens with planets. To the right of door no. 1 (bedroom), new vegetation begins and continues on panel 5.

Panel 5 (4 ft.) and panel 6 (6 ft.): These panels with no. 3 constitute the chief and highest surfaces of the overall mural. Panel 5: two palm trees and two deer, one large sun above door no. 2 (bedroom) on the right. Panel 6: two pronghorns below, one tall volcano above, regular branched tree with blue trunk, a leopard to the right.

Panel 7 (5 ft.): Door no. 3 (bathroom). On left, fish going upstream. On right, odd enigmatic black mask with staring eyes, a foot high. For me to try to describe the vividly delineated and surely varied colors throughout the mural would result in wasted effort. At least they deserve a mere mention, and thus I mention them. We might add some color photos to this account, but that can happen only much later. I await copies from a photographer friend.

As a separate item, lest we forget, I must relate the following story as reported to me by Jesse himself. This took place early after Muldoon Elder had established the Vorpal Gallery on the Embarcadero north of the Ferry Building in San Francisco, and after he had taken Jesse and his art on board for exposition there. The critic Alfred Frankenstein had come to the gallery to appraise the exhibit, including Jesse's own work. The artist just happened to visit the showroom at the same time by sheer coincidence, and evidently before the critic dismissed him in print as a mediocre painter.

One of the staff members, who happened to be present, remarked to Jesse that, since both critic and artist had come to the gallery simultaneously, they might as well meet, and he introduced them. The critic was in a hurry and had finished his appraisal. He simply acknowledged Jesse with a casual hello without looking him in the eye or shaking his hand. Had he bothered to talk with him, he might have been surprised at the depth and range of Jesse's own culture and cultivation in art, literature, and languages.

A Defense and Illustration of One Poetic Method

On June 16th, 1971, an esoteric Midwest publishing house, to wit, Arkham House of Sauk City, Wisconsin, under the owner-editorship of August Derleth, brought out a curious and esoteric book entitled *Songs and Sonnets Atlantean*. And certainly for the main mass of Anglo-American readers, Arkham House, despite its long-term tenacity, remains definitely esoteric, but more to the readers' loss than to that of the particular publishers. The present writer was the author-poet of that little volume and quite unintentionally "put one over" on the official bibliographical authorities.

On the official library card created for *Songs and Sonnets Atlantean* by the Library of Congress (Washington, D.C.), the author is listed merely as the "comp." (or "compiler"), and the book is classified as "1. French poetry—Translated into English. 2. English poetry—Translations from French." Yet only three poems are genuine translations from the French (that is, from the originals by three French poets definitely known to have existed) out of a total of 79 selections, whether in verse or in prose, with most of the selections by the official author or "compiler" himself. The three genuine French poets are Pierre de Ronsard, Louise Labé, and José-Maria de Heredia.

The five pieces *not* created (or at least re-created) by the official author himself (out of the total 79 selections) are: the sonnet to Edmund Spenser by "G. W. Senior, to the Author" quoted on the dedication page and beginning "Ah! Colin, whether on the lowly plain"; the sonnet "If music and sweet poetry agree" by Richard Barnfield but still attributed to Shakespeare on occasion; "To an Atlantean Poet" by Margo Skinner; "Inspiration" by Ian M. M. Law; and the sonnet "Secretest" by Fritz Leiber.

Considering the esoteric nature of the publishers involved, to say nothing of the esoteric nature of the book itself, it remains a source of amazement to its humble author that it should have attracted any attention and publicity at all, and that it should have gathered as much favorable reaction as it did, and as it continues to draw. Ignoring for the nonce the scholarly apparatus of the "Introduction" and "Notes" by one "Dr. Ibid Massachusetts Andor" (presently residing in the Azores), the volume reveals itself as an unabashedly romantic, old-fashioned, and aesthetic *trouvaille* of poetry in verse and in prose. What could have been more unlikely (on the surface of things) than *that,* at least in 1971? It had not been quite 400 years since the great Elizabethan adventure in poetry began with Spenser's first major work *The Shepheardes Calender* (completed and published in 1579), a particular tradition from which *Songs and Sonnets Atlantean* allegedly claims its literary descent and inspiration.

For those few and selective readers then who could see beyond the surface, the entire volume constituted somewhat an act of faith (or poetic faith, if you will) and an attempt to return to the roots of things, and relative to Spenser a return to the roots of the language and poetry in the "early modern period" of English literature, specifically back to *The Shepheardes Calender* and *The Faerie Queene.* All in all then, the book embodies (by way of an extended compliment, at least on one practical level) an elaborate ceremonial to respect and honor that man who (more than any other) deserves the historical appellation (if anyone does at all) of "the Father of Modern English Literature."

Again, considering the esoteric nature of the volume's publication, it remains a source of amazement that the book has attracted for the most part a favorable reaction. It has also attracted some negative or (at least) mixed response. Most notably perhaps, this mixed response is exemplified by Mark Purcell's by no means unfriendly notice appearing in that serious review of speculative fiction, *Luna Monthly,* for December 1972. Please see the Appendix for the entire text (in its original sequence) of Mr. Purcell's review, because herein we shall be making only isolated or partial quotations therefrom.

The following "defense" therefore owes its immediate impetus to what can be fairly accurately termed a "negative motivation," but also owes (by that very token) a considerable debt of gratitude to Mr. Purcell for existing at all. The reader is advised not to interpret or regard any development in the following "defense" or explication as critical of, or hostile to, anything stated by Mr. Purcell, who certainly has his own inalienable right to express any opinion whatsoever he wishes relative to *Songs and Sonnets Atlantean* or any other book. However, in the course of the review he does make a number of statements, allegations, or implications which, in view of the circumstances, might need or warrant some further emendation.

Furthermore, Mr. Purcell's review has indicated to the present writer the obvious need of making not only a logical "defense" of his little book (in terms of some of the specific statements the critic makes) but also the equally obvious need of appending some kind of "illustration," or some precise or articulated statement, of at least one (possible) poetic *working* method, such as turned out to be the author-poet's own during the decade of travail required to complete the opus in question.

And yet further, we must acknowledge *overall* a considerable debt of gratitude to both *Luna Monthly* and Mark Purcell, a magazine and a reviewer we appreciate and admire. Let us enumerate then. The author himself sent the copy of *Songs and Sonnets Atlantean* to be reviewed, and they responded quite nicely with a fair and most proper notice. The present writer wishes to thank Mark Purcell for writing, and *Luna Monthly* for publishing, such a proper notice, moreover one that is twice or three times the length of their average review. This is an honor and we do appreciate it, no irony or sarcasm intended or stated or covertly harbored!

The "illustration" will follow the "defense"—therefore please note the following specific "rebuttals" as well as commentary.

- "Some of the problems S&SA causes a reviewer can be explained by saying that it is the first book on the Atlantis legend in Renaissance France that can be recommended primarily to readers and librarians buying in the field of regional Californian verse: Sterling, Miss French, Clark Ashton Smith."

Granted, the book can cause any given reviewed divers and sundry problems, especially if it is not recognized at the outset that the book tells its own myth and/or creates its own world (in the time-honored tradition of much "speculative fiction"), and that the principal myth or mythos in turn details its own main narrative as any decent and "propriety"-respecting myth or story should.

Further, the "little booke" (to employ Don Herron's phrase) can cause any given reviewer serious problems if it is not also recognized at the outset that the overall text (including the dust-jacket blurbs) forms in its entirety a mode (however unusual) of storytelling (but truly fashioning an original "conceit" or "concetto") whereby the main narrative is hinted at or simply mentioned somewhere in the text (in this case, in the "Introduction" and in the "Notes"), and with the pieces of "poetry" themselves (whether in verse or in prose) acting as the main in-detail and in-depth units of mythic or literally mythopoeic focus.

This mode or method is essentially "modern" and even avant-garde (in certain recondite respects). Instead of the six or seven versions of the same story as proffered, say, by certain modern French novelists (or *antiromanciers*), the book tells one main story (with subsidiary traditions or narrative "threads" woven solidly into that main "tapestry") *but in the form* of a seemingly miscellaneous or random compilation of poems or "fragments"—and with some veritable "explications" presented *neutrally* in the volume's "frame" (that is, in the "Introduction" and the "Notes"). Thus, the reader must "work" to discover or recover the main narrative (to wit, "the romance of the Princess Aïs and the Prince Atlantarion"); but "clues" are scattered both carefully and abundantly over the entire "terrain" from the beginning of the book (including both its outer front dust-jacket and its inner front dust-jacket or flap) up though its conclusion (including the printer's note, the inner back dust-jacket or flap, and then the final and outer back dust-jacket featuring a photograph of the author-poet himself attired as "The Last of the Courtly Poets").

And thus the poems themselves, qua poems, are either isolated moments in that main narrative or (more subtly) tangential "reflections" or "extensions" or "extrapolations" from those isolated moments in the main narrative. And thus, further, the "Introduction" and "Notes" offer the "compiler" (yes, thus "officially" recognized) a "witty" and "pithy" opportunity to make observations upon the poems and *the nature of poetry in general* by creating a kind of dialectical commentary in an uniquely *self*-conscious and *self*-chosen style.

"I speak of this area as it existed before hard-boiled professional invaders like Jeffers, Winters and Rexroth invaded its backyard Pacific Coast culture and professionalized it."

There is the distinct implication here that whereas Robinson Jeffers, Yvor Winters, and Kenneth Rexroth are "professionals," then Sterling, French, and Smith must be "non-professionals." Although the West Coast artists were but rarely recognized and considered favorably by the East Coast critical establishment, they were known and respected by much of the English [i.e., Anglo-British] critico-literary fraternity from at least the 1870s onward (specifically the time of Ambrose Bierce's as well as Joaquin Miller's extended sojourns in England); and later the leading West Coast (San Francisco) periodicals (the *Argonaut, Town Talk,* etc.) were sold in both London and Paris. There is also the distinct implication here that whereas Jeffers, Winters, and Rexroth are "professional" (and hence "universal"), then Sterling, French, and Smith are only of "regional" interest (and thus not only "amateur" or "non-professional" but "provincial" as well). However, the facts of Californian literary history will testify to a different kind of story altogether.

"The golden sunlight of suburban, pre-smog, pre-sound-film California plays over Mr. Fryer's text."

If one deletes the word "suburban" (suburbia in our more recent sense virtually did not exist earlier in the twentieth century on the West Coast), this is an apt and original way of expressing it.

". . . Mr. Fryer purports to write a sequence of descriptive poems not about Plato's Atlantis but about a 13,000 B.C. Atlantean kingdom out beyond Gibraltar in 'our' Atlantic Ocean."

Really? On the contrary, Mr. Fryer very much does write about Plato's Atlantis. Has Mr. Purcell ever read either the *Timaeus* or the *Critias?* Plato clearly locates his island continent out beyond Gibraltar in what we today call the North Atlantic Ocean: he reports this as the main island kingdom (named Atlantis) which rules over nine lesser island kingdoms. Plato simply alludes to these in the *Timaeus,* but in the *Critias* he gives the names of their kings but without indicating the precise names and locations of the island kingdoms over which they reign beyond stating that they were islands, or groups of islands, lying in the open sea somewhat roundabout Atlantis or beyond it. In the "Introduction" and "Notes," "Dr. Andor" presumably identifies these divers island kingdoms with real island locales.

If one accepts Plato's Atlantis as fiction rather than an actual historical report, then the next logical step is to look for a genuine occurrence upon whose traditions the Greek philosopher-poet-fictioneer was consciously drawing when he put his two dialogues together. Thus, the eruption of Santorin (à la Krakatoa) in the southern Aegean Sea (north of Crete) has been recently cited as the original "Atlantis" cataclysm whose seismic waves [tsunamis] presumably destroyed at least the Minoan towns and cities on Crete's northern coast, as well as any communities on the pre-Hellenic island of Santorin. Now, all this would have constituted an "Atlantis" of sorts. Again, if we regard Plato's Atlantis as a fiction, then all this (Santorin and Crete) could have served as a "model" from which the Greek philosopher could have extrapolated his Atlantean Empire (mainly) into the North Atlantic Ocean. In other words, we must insist on the distinction between Plato's Atlantic-based Empire of Atlantis and whatever pre-Hellenic historical traditions or locales upon which he may have consciously drawn. The two concepts are by no means the same.

"This ocean had the bad taste to flood the kingdom over and leave only a few upthrusting seamarks (the Canaries, the Mariettas and Cape Verde Islands) as memorials to a ten-island kingdom stretching between Africa and the Americas."

The Madeiras, along with the Azores, the Canary Islands, the Cape Verde Islands, etc., are mentioned in the text, but not the Mariettas. The present writer has been unable to locate these last in any atlas or geography. Possibly Mr. Purcell is confusing them with the Marianas in the Pacific.

". . . This colonial empire was built on a huge pomegranate trade. . . ."

The commerce of and within "the Empire of Atlantis" was built on a variety of goods and products characteristically contributed by each island kingdom and not just on the "huge pomegranate trade" of Atkantharia.

"But as far as Mr. Fryer himself is concerned . . . *Songs and Sonnets Atlantean* only uses Atlantis for subject matter; the book is really a tribute to the Elizabethan (I) Edmund Spenser."

The book is really a variety of things or "threads," and whilst the continuous tribute to Spenser forms indeed a basic part of the overall concept, it is nonetheless *only one* part (out of many), and by no means exhausts the volume's fundamental *core* (or whatever it is the book is really about).

"Mr. Fryer considers himself an analogous Elizabethan (II) poet in style and content, with Atlantis equivalent to the Camelot of Spenser's *Faerie Queene*."

Mr. Fryer considers himself, if anything, a Neo-Elizabethan (i.e., pertaining to the Age of Elizabeth II). It is nowhere stated or even implied that he considers himself analogous to Spenser (he would not even dare to make such a presumption): however, he does count himself among the many poets in English who have derived technical and literally *poetic* inspiration from Spenser and *The Faerie Queene.*

If anything, Atlantis would be equivalent to the "Faerie land" of Spenser's *Faerie Queene.* There is no Camelot in his epic-romance-allegory (this would have been immediately contrary to the logic or "propriety" of the Arthurian Mythos he was fashioning), since Spenser treats of Arthur *as prince before he became king.*

The "great city" in *The Faerie Queene* is Cleopolis (where Queen Gloriana rules in high splendor), also called "Troynovant" on at least one occasion, and suggestive of London in a number of specific details or "properties." Thus, Gloriana's crystal tower-palace Panthèa is evidently modelled after the Tower of London.

"For his key sonnet sequence (I–XVII, pp. 78–94), Mr. Fryer has expanded FQ's famous stanza form to create a new type of sonnet . . . [partially] depending on some private Elizabethan code."

Not bad; a good try; but not quite exact! Mr. Fryer has developed Spenser's *sonnet* form by "shewing forth" the Spenserian stanza (the stanza employed in *The Faerie Queene*) latent within it, and then by arranging the five lines remaining as a tercet and a couplet. This resultant Spenserian stanza-sonnet is, moreover, a perfectly logical development of, or from, the given prosody, and in no way depends "on some private Elizabethan code."

In any case, it does exemplify the author-poet's own original contribution to English-language prosody, and it does demonstrate that the older prosody is by no means exhausted if it can definitely show such further innovations.

"What is Sterling-Californian, not Spenser-English, is Mr. Fryer's refusal to devise an Atlantean story-poem like Spenser's Arthurian *Queene.*"

Mr. Fryer has not *refused* "to devise an Atlantean story-poem like Spenser's Arthurian *Queene.*" Instead, Mr. Fryer has decided to do something else (as detailed at the beginning of the present "defense"):

to tell one main story arranged as a presumably random sequence of pieces (or parts) in prose and in verse.

However, it is not at all clear how or why Mr. Fryer's "refusal to devise an Atlantean story-poem" is explicitly Sterling-Californian, not Spenser-English. This is a non sequitur, and is demonstrably untrue in regard to the early twentieth-century Northern Californian poetic tradition.

Sterling, Nora May French, Ashton Smith, Ambrose Bierce, etc., were all quite capable of telling (or subtly implying) a story in verse.

Incidentally, there is a real historical connection between Sterling's California and Spenser's England. The reader is referred to the last part of this article for details. [This connection involves Sir Francis Drake, Nova Albion, June-July 1579.]

"Mr. Fryer has the 'modern' (post-Wordsworth) belief in descriptive landscape poetry."

Mr. Fryer's use of and/or belief in descriptive landscape poetry owes virtually nothing to the "'modern' (post-Wordsworth)" tradition. It stems instead, and primarily, from a close reading (first) in the poetry of the French Renaissance (specifically the poems created by the Pléiade, and especially *Les Antiquités de Rome* and other sonnet-sequences by Joachim du Bellay), and (second) in the poetry of the English Renaissance.

"Spenser took more interest in telling verse-stories or in the psychological arguments of his Platonic hymns and of his sonnet sequence, 'Amoretti.'"

Spenser took more or most interest simply and foremost in creating his poetry, and all his other directions and purposes depends upon that first (or "primal") desire and cause. It might be a trifle more accurate to say that he took more interest, in regard to his Platonic hymns (of love and beauty and then of heavenly love and beauty), in their *metaphysical* arguments. It goes almost without saying that Spenser is always a keen and powerful "Psyche-ologist."

"But Mr. Fryer has nothing to say in his poems."

Thus, the accompanying essays in this especial romantic/fantasy issue [of *Nyctalops* for April 1976, double issue No. 11-12] might seem to indicate otherwise. However, if he does have something to say, Mr. Purcell at least does not perceive it.

"This is reflected in the deflating form of his sonnets. . . ."

In view of the fact that in their most characteristic form Mr. Fryer's Spenserian stanza-sonnets have their tercets and their couplets arranged as alexandrines or fourteeners (and thus longer than the usual iambic pentameter), it would be more accurate to refer to them as "afflating" rather than "deflating." If a given line (thus conceived in terms of traditional metrics) is longer than usual, then the reader, in vocalizing it, must take a deeper breath to project the given vocables adequately: hence, *afflatus* rather than *deflatus*.

"Both the orthodox English patterns make the conclusion structurally more important, whether in the octet argument of 8-6 or in the snapper-couplet of 4-4-4-2."

The *logos* (or logic) of the two or three main Elizabethan sonnet-forms (Petrarchan, Shakespearian, or Spenserian)—yes—does make the conclusion structurally more important, especially when the conclusion takes the shape of a rhyming couplet, whether cast in iambic pentameter or in a longer line. Mr. Fryer was indeed quite well aware of this, and took full advantage of it in devising his own sonnet-form.

"(Mr. Fryer's couplet conclusions are more relaxed and metrically longer.)"

Almost from the start of that particular period of time when he was inventing his own sonnet, Mr. Fryer realized that for his purposes the concluding couplet (at least) needed to be longer than the usual iambic pentameter. Later, he realized that the tercet also needed to be longer in order to carry the Spenserian stanza-sonnet to its concluding phase of logical development.

If Mr. Purcell "hears" Mr. Fryer's couplet-conclusions as "more relaxed," then that is indeed *his* own ear, to which he is of course completely welcome.

"The strict prose sense in Fryer's poems is banal."

Again, the accompanying essays in this especial romance/fantasy issue of *Nyctalops* might seem to indicate otherwise.

"What he wishes, is of course the mellifluousness of the Surrey tradition in Elizabethan (I) poetry, to which Spenser and Marlowe contributed; and to which contemporary poets [i.e., of the twentieth century] like Perse, Stevens and Hart Crane still belong."

Mr. Purcell is exaggerating the importance of the Surrey tradition in Elizabethan poetry. One cannot deny the importance of Wyatt and Surrey's poetry published in *Tottel's Miscellany* in 1557. Surrey in particular naturalized both the sonnet and blank verse in English. Surrey's sonnets, rather than those of Wyatt, exercised a genuine influence on Sir Philip Sidney and other Elizabethan poets. The true Elizabethan tradition of characteristic "mellifluousness" did not find its inauguration until the publication of *The Shepheardes Calendar* in 1579. This first book by Spenser as a mature poet began the Elizabethan efflorescence of poetry and song; exercised a profound influence on virtually all contemporary and subsequent English poets; and was reprinted many times in Spenser's lifetime, an honor not accorded to just any book, not at that period in the history of printing and publishing.

"But the sonnet was invented as a form, back in Italy, not so much for pretty writing, but to express difficulties and tensions."

The sonnet was *one* important development in the evolution of (early) modern European prosody, and in particular derived from the songs and poems of the troubadours, trouvères, etc. One staple theme of their work was the praise of the belovèd or beautiful one (the woman lover), and a special rhetoric or convention of praise in the various vernacular languages developed (with its original roots in the study of Latin, Greek, and Hebrew classics). Thus, the tradition of literally beauty-full language, or "pretty writing" (as Mr. Purcell expresses it), had a long-established precedent, and thus came into being before what was to become the later stage involved in expressing "difficulties and tensions."

"It wasn't a technically demanding form in Italian, no matter what American high school teachers say about it now."

While it may not have been an especially strict form in Italian (although it never does right to underestimate the technical difficulties of any given poetic forms in the romance languages), the sonnet has certainly proven such for the most part in English, which is of course a rime-poor language compared to French, Spanish, Latin, etc. This was formerly true of English literature even in the Elizabethan Age, which allowed a far greater prosodic and syntactic freedom than what presently obtains.

"Compared to its source form, the difficult sestina, sonnets are almost free verse." (Not quite!)

Whatever its source form, and no matter the difficulty of the sestina, or that "sonnets are almost free verse" (not quite!), the sonnet, or a standard stanza-form such as the Spenserian, has a descriptive and/or narrative suitability which in many strategic instances makes it the more appropriate or "proper" aesthetic form than the sestina.

What is important in this particular case is not the difficulty of the form chosen to be one of the main vehicles of narrative or descriptive projection, but its aesthetic aptness or "propriety" (as understood in the terms of Renaissance literary criticism).

"The interesting early English sonnets grew not from the Surrey tradition but from Sir Thomas Wyatt (Sidney-Donne-the dramatist Shakespeare), and many of these sonneteers were considered metrically rough, coarse writers."

The fame and interest attendant on the publication of *Astrophel and Stella* (the sequence of songs and sonnets by Sir Philip Sidney) proved to be the single greatest influence (first circulated extensively in manuscript) on other Elizabethan poets in regard to cultivating this especial form. We should interpolate here that literary people then and now consider Sidney's own sequence notably suave and aesthetic, just the opposite of rough or coarse. The mellifluousness of the language does not impair in any way the intellectual interest of the poetry.

Sidney's work would have stimulated particularly Spenser on the one hand and Shakespeare on the other.

"Sweet Will" (it must not be forgotten) was first and principally esteemed among the literary arbiters of his day, less for his plays and much more for such euphonious narratives as *Venus and Adonis* and *The Rape of Lucrece,* as well as for his "sugared sonnets." Even at that time poets were still considered (in terms of their public or "forensic" image) "sweet singers." Their tradition was still above all else that of the troubadours and minnesingers (those grave and serious lyricists whose greatest effusions characteristically rhapsodized the beauty, grace, and compassion of the Virgin Mary). Purely poetic songs and sonnets were set to music, and some poets would improvise on the lute while extemporizing or reciting any given verses. Thus, the so-called cliché "the bardic lute" refers to an historical and practical reality.

"Historically, there has always been some famous poet in English who could turn out a good example of the form, but it is perhaps significant that since Milton the greatest technicians (Pope, Tennyson, Eliot) have been bored by the form."

The present writer would expand Mr. Purcell's trinity to include at least these other figures as excellent sonneteer-technicians: the English Romantic poets, Longfellow, Swinburne, George Sterling, Ashton Smith, and others. Many of the latter indubitably became acknowledged masters of the standard sonnet-forms or innovated their own versions of the same. Many contemporary poets continue to create sonnets.

"Mr. Fryer must be the only poet to have listened to *Green Sleeves* (p. 67)—OK, Vaughan Williams' *Fantasia*—and not try to write words that fit the melody."

Since Mr. Purcell assures the reader that "the strict prose sense in Fryer's poems is banal," Mr. Fryer confesses himself somewhat amazed at the imaginative modesty (on Mr. Purcell's part) apropos of his creative stricture anent *Green Sleeves*. He wonders if it might not have dawned upon Mr. Purcell that the author may have been deliberately trying to do something other than what Mr. Purcell suggests. In point of fact, the author-poet was only trying to capture within the logic of his own sonnet-form (aspiring to do full justice to the form's own Spenserian antecedents) something—a *selective* something—of the sense of the long-breathédness in the original melody, particularly when heard in Vaughan Williams's profound realization of the tune. Its deliberately slow-paced sense (and *not* strict tempo) of melody is all (technically) the poet was consciously trying to imitate (again, *selectively*). The poet certainly did not have as his own creative ambition anything so literal (and ultimately so futile) as attempting to fit words to the preconceived melody of *Green Sleeves*. Again, the poem (using its own musico-poetic means) essays only a kind of "dialectical" (and surely "aesthetic") commentary upon the original melody: simply, as aesthetic appreciation, or a conceit of compliments.

"To write in the sonnet form about *Green Sleeves* suggests a coarse ear."

If in Mr. Purcell's own terms, even after the explication given above, Mr. Fryer still has a coarse ear, then so be it, and let Mr. Purcell's Rhadamanthus-like judgment abide!

* * *

The "defense" now rests, and the "illustration" (which may be stated more compactly) proceeds apace.

During the decade of sustained effort and work required to complete it, the author-poet created *Songs and Sonnets Atlantean* according to a precise working method, that is, in accordance (literally) with a musical analogy. Thus, the various major divisions or sections of the book, the author conceived in terms as of "movements"—as in a suite or symphony, only in this case an unconventional number of movements, say, six or seven, as in the "Ocean" or "Dramatic" Symphonies by Anton Rubinstein.

Thus, the lengthy "Introduction" (the first movement) literally serves as a grand introduction into the main body of the overall work, announcing the various "themes" and "counterthemes." Then, the second movement takes the form of the first major presentation of verse-poems (like the book, entitled *Songs and Sonnets Atlantean*). Next, the "Minor Chronicles of Atlantis" (a series of twelve prose-poems) makes up the third movement. Then, a series of Spenserian stanza-sonnets and of Spenserian stanzas (regularly alternating) embodies the fourth movement. Subsequently, the (seventeen) "Sonnets on an Empire of Many Waters" form the fifth movement. And then the sixth movement (forming a major transition) consists of the dedicatory and commendatory verses by the author-poet as well as by other poets. The grand finale comes at last in the seventh and final movement; this forms a kind of reprise-finale, and thus a new "synthetic" *gallimaufry* of previous themes, counterthemes, etc. (that is, the "Notes"). Thus, the overall analogy is clearly to a kind of "polyphonic" work, cast in divers and sundry movements.

Even the very preliminary pages of this book-long (architectural) "conceit" serve as a kind of preliminary introduction preparatory (or "warming up") to the next and major introduction proper. Thus, the first title page, then the copyright and credits page, next the second title page, the acknowledgments page, the dedication page, the (three) contents pages (mark that three!), and so forth, are analogous to preliminary fanfaronades or flourishes for trumpets.

Thus, the various poems in verse (cast in some version of Spenser's own stanza or stanza-form) might be seen (within each major section or movement) as a kind of variation-technique at work, with each poem embodying one given variation in or of the overall (potential) *poetic* melody. To press the overall musical analogy further, the author-poet deliberately chose the two principal prosodic forms for their previously established *musical* character and potential. Thus we have the already highly "musical" Spenserian stanza. Thus we have also the highly "musical" Spenserian sonnet-form, made even more "musical" by developing the Spenserian stanza latent within it, and by arranging the five final lines (the tercet and the couplet) as lines longer than the usual pentameter. Hence, note the further prolongation of purely poetic melody now made possible by the simple aggrandizement or elongation of those particular lines.

Thus, in the Spenserian stanza-sonnet as presented in its most developed or characteristic form (as, for example, in the "Sonnets on an Empire of Many Waters"), we have still further the rondeau-like device whereby line 3 more or less repeats as line 13, and line 1 as line 14, all proportions guarded. ("Through this device, amongst others, Mr. Fryer hopes to restore to the sonnet or *sonetto*—that is, 'little song' in Italian—some of its original, purely *singing,* qualities.") What could possibly be more emphatic than that?—whether in terms of a musical analogy, or in terms of a broadly conceived "clue" or "key" for the benefit of a given reader in understanding (in part) the book's overall "system."

Then (finally), in consideration of the book's purely musical "mathematics" (or mystical numerologies}, there is the particular emphasis on such numerals as 3, 4, 5, 7, 9, 10, and 17. In the event that the overall musical analogy (according to which the book was conceived) might pass unnoticed by the reader, obvious or "punning" clues are placed in the most *e*xposed locations. Thus, the very title of the book itself ("songs and sonnets," that is, songs and little songs) is reiterated over and over (at the top of the pages); and then the title for the final section (to wit, "Notes") could not make the musical analogy any more evident than what it is!

Before we continue, we must detail something of the real historical connection between Sterling's California and Spenser's England, or to put it more appositely, between Britain and California in the Age of Elizabeth I. And this "genuine, real, authentic" historical connection comes in via none other than Francis Drake (but knighted later) and his globe-circumnavigating ship, the *Golden Hinde*.

It is not a generally well-known fact (at least not in the form that we now present), but it is nonetheless a fact, that the original "New England" (although not a permanent colony) was first proclaimed by the English in Northern California in 1579. During his original circumnavigation of the planet (December 1577 into September 1580), before sailing westward across the Pacific Ocean, Drake had been voyaging north along the western coast of the Spanish Americas, looking for a passage to the Atlantic. He sailed as far as latitude 48° North (possibly somewhere around Vancouver Island), but bitterly cold weather forced the *Golden Hinde* southward. The English were no strangers to bitterly cold weather, given their own England in winter.

Drake sailed back along the Oregon coast. The ship was leaking and needed a protected anchorage for repairs. At latitude 38° North, Drake put into a "faire and good Baye" some 30 or 40 miles north or northwest of modern San Francisco. This was on 17 June 1579, according to the famous "plate of brass" found in Marin County back in the 1930s, and still not accepted as evidence by some discriminating historians. He more than likely landed at what is today Drake's Bay, or Drake's Estero, on the south or southwest of the Point Reyes Peninsula. The English found the Coastal Miwok Indians friendly and cooperative, and relations between them apparently proved cordial.

Drake gave the name of Nova Albion—that is New Albion, or "New England" (from Albion, the ancient poetic or mythological name for England)—to the California coast because of the white "cliffs" (or great white sand dunes) near his landfall, similar in general appearance to the white cliffs of Dover. Thus, the English took possession of the (at least) Northern California coastland in the name of the first Queen Elizabeth. The territory claimed by Drake would have included, of course, the present-day Marin County, not to mention San Francisco Bay to the south, which the English apparently did not discover at that time. Incredibly thick fogs evidently masked the entrance to the great inland body of water.

After thirty-seven days in Nova Albion, and with the repairs to the *Golden Hinde* completed, the English put to sea again from Drake's Bay, saying farewell to the amicable Miwok Indians, and headed southwest across the Northern Pacific Ocean, continuing on back toward England. Drake's former anchorage is manifested as "Portus Novae Albionis" on the rare Judocus Hondius world map of 1589, which traces Drake's circumnavigation, thus ten years after his landfall on the California coast.

But virtually at one and the same time, whilst Francis Drake was achieving one of the high points in the great Elizabethan adventure of discovery and exploration (and particularly whilst he was provisionally setting up the first "New England"), Edmund Spenser was inaugurating the great Elizabethan adventure in poetry (considered the chief of all the arts at that time, including music and literature) with his first major work, *The Shepheardes Calender,* completed and published in 1579. Spenser had finished his *Calender* in its entirety by 10 April 1579. It was entered in the Stationers' Register in London on 5 December and was published soon thereafter in that same month under the pseudonym of "Immerito." This work had circulated widely before publication (marking the true Elizabethan efflorescence of poetry and song) and exercised a profound and lasting influence on almost all contemporary and subsequent poets.

From this particular tradition *Songs and Sonnets Atlantean* has claimed and still claims its literary descent and inspiration (even if not quite to the same extent as it does from *The Faerie Queene*). It had not been quite 400 years since Spenser had finished his first major opus, and since Francis Drake had put ashore in the original "New England" on the California coast, when *Songs and Sonnets Atlantean* finally appeared in published form on 16 June 1971. It had thus appeared one day earlier than 17 June 1579, when the English first landed among the Coastal Miwok Indians.

The book's formal dedication reads in all seriousness and sincerity: DEDICATED, / IN THIS THE REIGN OF ELIZABETH II, / TO THE MEMORY OF EDMUND SPENSER, / POET LAUREATE TO ELIZABETH I. Again, not quite 400 years after Drake, the first Renaissance Pleasure Faire (the first of its type anywhere in the U.S. or the U.K.) opened in 1967 just outside the city of San Rafael, Marin County (again north of San Francisco), not very far from the site of Drake's original landfall and campsite, say, perhaps 25 miles east as the bird flies. The Faire (sponsored by the incorporated

Renaissance Centre with its headquarters in San Francisco) celebrated its ninth anniversary in 1975. It has always taken place in a choice and picturesque oak forest of some considerable description, and the Centre will evidently erect an Elizabethan or Renaissance Village of a permanent nature which will function as an enriching medium between the old Renaissance and the Neo-Renaissance (as prompted in a sense by the reign of Elizabeth II), and where a new Renaissance Centre will arise. [Per the last report the Centre now has its home in Gilroy, about 25 miles inland east of Santa Cruz, the latter at the northern end of Monterey Bay.]

Over 30 years after "Nova Albion," the English proclaimed the second (and lasting) New England in that area which has thus been called ever since. New England is an Atlantic coastal region in the northeastern U.S., and comprises the states of Massachusetts, Connecticut, Rhode Island, New Hampshire, Vermont, and Maine (originally a part of Massachusetts). While politically a part of New York State, geographically Long Island is really a part of New England. Officially it was first called a newer Albion in 1614 by Captain John Smith. During his voyage of 1614, Smith had applied this name to the region in question, and he significantly entitled his subsequent book *A Description of New England* (1616). The name was obvious enough, since a New Spain and a New France (Canada) already existed. Smith certainly knew that Drake had named the Northern California coast New Albion or "New England." A memory of that particular naming accounts for the later naming of the Albion River and the town of Albion at its mouth, as thus called by a romantically minded Englishman in 1844. (The Albion River flows into the Pacific south of Mendocino, and about 100 miles northwest of San Francisco.)

It is curious that Drake was as struck by the white "cliffs" (or great white sand dunes) near his landfall on the California coast (similar in general appearance to the white cliffs of Dover), as earlier the Romans had been by the chalk cliffs that still bear that name, when they had first landed there. Drake was indeed sufficiently struck to affix the name of Nova Albion to that patch of Elizabethan California which he and his men inhabited for more than thirty days.

Albion had evidently served as the ancient name for the island of Britain. Thus, Avienus quotes Massilote Periplus of the sixth century

B.C.E. who mentions "the island of the Albiones," and other Greek geographers not only distinguish Albion from Ierne (or Ireland) and from smaller "Britannic" islands but also maintain that Albion was the native appellation. This has been translated as "white land"—and the Romans explained this as referring to the white chalk cliffs of Dover, comparing the name to the Latin "albus" or white.

Of course it was inevitable that the later Californian "Anglos"— especially the New Englanders and the English who came to California during the Gold Rush of the late 1840s and early 1850s—should have invoked the earlier historical connection between Britain and California in the Age of Elizabeth I, a connection they would have perceived quite properly (in their own romantic way) as the quintessence of romance indeed.

As part of this early "Anglo" romanticism, we must cite Eulalie (Mary Eulalie Fee, 1824-1854, originally of New Richmond, Ohio), California's first woman poet in English, who flourished but a poignantly brief period of time as "the Auburn Poetess" in the Auburn and Sacramento area, from the early spring of 1854 to the early winter of the same year, when she died in childbirth in late December. Her best poems reveal her as a careful craftswoman with a delicate, if not refined, romantic sensibility. In her own modest way Eulalie anticipates the work of such East Coast poets as Emily Dickinson and Edna St. Vincent Millay, in addition to beginning a West Coast tradition continued by Ina Donna Coolbrith, Nora May French, Susan Myra Gregory, and so forth, a tradition somewhat analogous to that of Dickinson and Millay on the opposite side of the continent.

This "retiring and idealistic" poet was "the object of pride, love, and interest to hundreds of young mining adventurers . . . and her fame became wide in the mines." (An old resident of the Auburn area thus recalls her.) Eulalie made a decisive contribution to the earliest Californian "Anglo" Romanticism as much by her gently charismatic figure as by her own poems. Steeped in the conventional pieties of her time about nature and human life, her work reveals no great imagination or distinctive originality, as does the poetry of Nora May French. In virtually all respects the influence of the Anglo-Americans on the Hispanic California of the mid-1800s proved overwhelming in both the political and the cultural spheres. By the 1880s and the 1890s the city of San Francisco had become the cultural and financial capital of the West Coast, with her own adopted Ambrose Bierce as possibly her single greatest literary and critical "big wheel."

Ah! "Bitter Bierce"—who carried almost as large a satiric mace as Jonathan Swift, who could write on one hand a perfect piece of sociopolitical satire in verse with a real impact, and who could then indite on the other hand an intimate sonnet to some lady-love, a sonnet that remains a little masterpiece of imaginative passion and fastidious delicacy, and surely of romanticism "all compact." The imaginative and poetic theories that "the Devil's Lexicographer" (so called on occasion) promulgated from time to time had everything to do with that final flowering of the Anglo-American "Romantic" school—that particular group of poets and prose-poets whom we might label with equal cause either as the California Late Romantics or as the California Modern Romantics—a group that included at least Bierce himself, Herman Scheffauer, George Sterling, Nora May French, Ashton Smith, as well as other poets and writers.

Nor must it be forgotten that Sterling in his own turn helped and encouraged a great many poets, and would often do all that he could to bring financial aid (as well as official and critical recognition) to remarkable talent or genius. H. P. Lovecraft, Ashton Smith, H. L. Mencken, and others in their turn perceived Sterling as the foremost living (and "public") poet in the American classical-romantic tradition during the second and third decades of the twentieth century. Sterling was unstinting in the financial and critical assistance he was often able to gather for the younger Ashton Smith, whom the elder poet clearly recognized as a genius rare in any generation.

The prefaces that Sterling contributed to Smith's *Odes and Sonnets* (1918) and *Ebony and Crystal* (1922) are models of compact appreciation, and surely quintessential in their informed sense of imagination and wonder and cosmic-astronomic-mindedness. Sterling also recognized (before his own death) the unique and epochal genius of the modern cosmic poet Robinson Jeffers, who started off on his official Californian career under the aegis (and with the approval) of the elder poet. All these three figures, Sterling, Smith, and Jeffers, stand out for the conspicuous cosmic edge in their best work.

We can bracket circa 1890 to 1960/61 as the definitive period under discussion, with 1890 to 1926/30 and 1926/30 to 1960/61 as the two main subperiods. Circa 1890 on into 1914 turned out to be Bierce's final and greatest period of influence. Born in 1881, Nora May French was especially active as a poet (published in Californian periodicals) from about the *fin-de-siècle* until her tragic death in November 1907. Born in 1869, Sterling began his major creativity as a poet at the start of the 1890s and was active until his death in November 1926; but he had been recognized as the unofficial poet laureate of San Francisco and the West Coast from late 1907 with the magazine appearance of *A Wine of Wizardry*. Born in 1876 or 1878 (both years are given), the German-born Herman Scheffauer died in Berlin in 1927. Incidentally, Sterling and Scheffauer were Bierce's two favorite and most remarkable poet-pupils.

Born in 1893, and influenced by both Bierce and Sterling, Clark Ashton Smith (now virtually alone) kept his unique heritage from the older California Romantics alive after Sterling's death—he and Bierce had functioned above all as the most conspicuous figures in the group—and especially during that ill-defined but major shift in public and critical taste from the middle to the later 1920s onward. Recognized by Sterling as a greater poet than himself, Smith and his four collections of verse—*The Star-Treader* (1912), *Odes and Sonnets* (1918), *Ebony and Crystal* (1922), and *Sandalwood* (1925)—represent the finest expression of the Californian school of "pure poetry." Thanks to Sterling, he found critical recognition through the San Francisco press, which created his first major audience. Later Sterling expanded that audience when he would appear in Manhattan before poets and critical pontiffs. During the 1930s Smith discovered and maintained his second major audience for his unusual Muse through the pages of "The Unique Magazine"—to wit, *Weird Tales*—to which he contributed many of his inimitable short stories. During the 1940s he returned almost completely to the creation of poetry, and the 1950s witnessed principally a well-earned retirement through marriage in Pacific Grove on the Monterey Peninsula.

We can cite, as two of the chief stylistic ingredients in the overall *oeuvre* of the California Romantics, rarity of imagination or imaginative concept—often with a cosmic or cosmic-astronomic element emphasized—and recondite vocabulary (consisting often enough of unusual and/or archaic words). All these linguistic tendencies are carried to an exotic perfection of form (in both verse and prose) in the epochal poetry and the outré prose fantasies of Ashton Smith, once hailed in the San Francisco press as the Poe and/or Baudelaire of California. Incidentally, he pushes on into a new realm of inspired reference and cosmic speculation, a rich and baroque prose that equals or out-baroques the "Baroque Glory" of Sir Thomas Browne. In particular, Smith sums up with rare finesse the use (by the California Romantics) of historically descended and now literally archaic words and phrases, often of Elizabethan, Jacobean, or occult vintage.

Furthermore, the inspired and integrated *modern* romanticism of the California Romantics is a tradition that lives on in various individual poets and other figures who either personally knew Sterling and Smith, who met with them on a number of strategic occasions, or who befriended them over a conspicuous period of time. Thus the gardener and literary connoisseur George Haas of Oakland, who often visited Smith in Pacific Grove and became Smith's single best friend in the latter's terminal decade of life (that is, apart from Smith's wife, of course). Thus the history professor William Farmer (but also expert in poetry and theology), who during his young adulthood virtually camped out at Smith's home near Monterey in the course of the latter's final years (as William once confided to the present writer). Thus the present author-poet, who visited Smith and his wife Carol Jones Dorman on two different occasions (late August 1958 and early September 1959), had some correspondence with him, and was able to render him some useful service before Smith died in August 1961.

From Spring 1960 to Summer 1965 the present writer compiled most of the materials for *Emperor of Dreams: A Clark Ashton Smith Bibliography* (published by Donald M. Grant, West Kingston, R.I., 1978), besides doing other necessary things for Smith's life and varied arts. From Spring 1961 to Spring 1971, the present writer was actively engaged in the creation of the First Series of his own *Songs and Sonnets Atlantean* (Arkham House, 1971), which grew directly out of the tail-end of the California Modern Romantic tradition—a tradition that seemed to the author at the time as only the lingering vestiges of an otherwise irrevocably lost Atlantis.

From Autumn 1965 to Spring 1971 the unique romanticism of

San Francisco, possibly the most romantic city in the world (especially since romanticism as an actively creative force *in Vienna* has been dead since World War II more or less, if not before then), has directly and additionally inspired as well as nourished the present writer's own poetic vision. What significantly held him and enchanted him there was the City's wealth of remaining Victorian mansions, palaces, and other buildings of the same and later periods. Her pervading sense of "otherness" and "otherwhere" (almost in a curiously Keltic sense), potent even today in the 1970s and later, has been wonderfully captured in a simple and yet classic manner in the lyric "San Francisco" as perpetrated by one G. Sutton Breiding, the young "modern romantic" poet and prose-poet (and *extra* anyone's *ordinary*), and resident for many years in the City by the Golden Gate. [G. Sutton Breiding returned in Summer 1986 to live in his native city of Morgantown, West Virginia.]

As a perfectly logical consequence of the mid-nineteenth-century romanticism of the Anglo-Americans, the small city of Avalon on Catalina Island bears the same name as the original (British) Isle of Avalon (per Geoffrey Ashe, the site of Glastonbury Abbey, Somerset, England). In the Excelsior District of San Francisco there is an Avalon Street, named not after the British Avalon-Glastonbury but after the city of Avalon on Catalina in the Pacific Ocean just west of the Los Angeles area.

Then the final and in some respects the most important direct link to the present writer's own immediate poetic tradition came via the auspices of the scholar and researcher Randal Alain Kirsch Everts, who introduced him (first through letters and then shortly after that through a personal visit) to Helen Augusta (French) Hunt, then the still surviving sister of Nora May French. This was in late Spring 1968. A singularly beautiful person and surely a remarkable woman quite apart from her gifted poet-sister, Helen French Hunt brought an entire earlier world of California's "Bohemia" to life, whether centered in San Francisco or on the Monterey Peninsula. Through her visits to the San Francisco Bay Area once or twice a year, but more abundantly through her warm and incisive correspondence, she put the present writer immediately in touch with California's *fin-de-siècle* and with its direct aftermath. She "humanized" his grasp of his own immediate poetic tradition, and she brought him closer to her dear sister Nora May, or "Phyllis," as she had become known in various circles in Los Angeles and San Francisco—this was the name that she adopted whilst living in the Los Angeles area.

But far more than that, Helen became a valued and uniquely dear friend who gave inspiration, encouragement, personal criticism, and on frequent occasions monetary assistance to the present writer. He discovered after her death in April 1973 that she had thus helped other young persons over the years—nor were they all struggling poets and beginning writers! Also after her death (on 9 April 1973: had she lived on into the summer, she would have been ninety on that subsequent 4 August, her birthday), some of her closest relatives mailed the present writer a small box of memorabilia, left to him by Helen as a bequest, largely relative to Nora May French and recalling the tragic circumstances of Nora May's death.

Here were letters to, from, and about Nora May. Here were photos of her as an adolescent and adult in California, as well as of her family. Here were photos of herself as a child, and of her family while still living in Aurora, New York, before they all moved to Southern California. Here was a poem written in her own hand, to wit, "Poppies." Here was a letter from George Sterling with a draft of his first and best memorial poem to Nora May, the sonnet that begins "I saw the shaken stars of midnight stir," a piece especially cherished by Helen. And here, perhaps most moving of all, and truly magical, the sterling silver napkin-ring, with an elegant Art Nouveau design of mermaids on either side of a scallop-type shell. In the middle of this is engraved the single name of Nora, who had used the napkin-ring as a child as well as later in Los Angeles.

[D. Sidney-Fryer later donated this small cache of memorabilia to the Bancroft Library, University of California, Berkeley. The donation was made under the aegis of D. Steven Black, Head of Acquisitions at the Bancroft.]

Thus, these are all some of the major links between *Songs and Sonnets Atlantean* (the First Series) and the Californian Late Romantic or Modern Romantic literary movement, which the book in part commemorates. The link between Amerindian California and Elizabethan Britain (June–July 1579) had long agone been established and had then been apparently forgotten. When *Songs and Sonnets Atlantean* was first published in June 1971 (almost 400 years later), the book with its dedication to Spenser's memory, and with its emphasis on the Spenserian tradition, made the symbolic gesture of pointing the Californian Late Romantic or Modern Romantic tradition back to its ultimate lyric and epic source in Early Modern English.

In consideration of the large role played in Californian history at the time of the Gold Rush by both the English and the New Englanders, we need only add that our author-poet hails originally from New England (specifically from New Bedford, southeastern Massachusetts), and not far from that Sag Harbor (say, about 75 miles as the bird flies), Long Island, where George Sterling was born and raised.

[N.B. This essay first appeared in the double issue, Nos. 11-12, of *Nyctalops,* that is, for April 1976. The poet-author has reproduced it here more or less as Harry O. Morris, the owner-editor, published it in Spring 1976. The essayist has however subjected the essay's latter half to some slight revision and addition. He has indicated these later addenda, made in February 2017, by enclosing them in brackets. The full text of Mark Purcell's review-notice of *Songs and Sonnets Atlantean* (the First Series)—in its original sequence and from its first appearance in *Luna Monthly* for December 1972—makes its (re)appearance in the appropriate appendix at the end of this book, following its second appearance in the issue of *Nyctalops* for April 1976.]

San Francisco

by G. Sutton Breiding

San Francisco
I only love you for
your mystery.
I love your greyblue fog
& pauseless seakissed winds,
your palaces & fallen mansions,
your secret maze of
lost & tangled streets,
your haunted nameless monuments
that stand like signals
from another world.

I love you for the quiet spots
within your depths
For the dreams that you
induce in me,
not the hard realities
that dull your beauty
with pretentious sham and glitter.

Old Frisco,
I think it's but the corpse of you
I love—
The rotting remnant
of a former time,
like ragged lace hanging
in the windows of decrepit
gabled towers—
the echoes of a greater splendour,
a humbler hour,
when you were sweeter, softer,
a young, resplendent city

by the pearlling bay
& wiser in your youth.

Now, in the surge of demon progress,
you more & more become a tomb,
filled with drunken zombies
with hordes of modern vampires
sucking the dreams from your blood,
leaving but a husk
corrupt & floundering
in its own senescence.

Go die then, San Francisco
Herb Caen will note your death in passing
to make another hundred grand.
Until I leave you once again,
I'll drift about your streets
in search eternally of mystery,
with the wind & fog-shrouded lamps my guides;
I'll go search out you evanescent beauties—
your swiftly fading romance
that lingers still about your weary limbs.

A few more times before I leave you
for another, I want to climb a lonely
hilltop, amidst a spired grove
& with a lady fair watch the sun set
far into the blue Atlantean waves . . .
—to see the heavy mist sweep
down & blanket you and then return to
my room & my wine,
to dream . . . & sleep with you once more . . .
before I disappear again
from your crumbling doorstep,
in search of different dreams,
& younger-hearted lovers.

A Note on History and/or Historiography

Story, history, historiography. The three words are all closely related, but do not mean quite the same thing. Story as a narration, a tale, an anecdote, an episode, or what have you, may take almost any form or shape in verse or in prose. History as a systematic, usually chronological narrative may concern itself with almost any phenomenon or thing, human-related or not, whether as *A History of Safety Pins* or *A History of the Antarctic Republic under the Penguins.* The French use *histoire* interchangeably to mean story or history, but the context generally makes the meaning clear, as in "I have a story to tell you," or *A History of French Literature from the Renaissance up to the First World War.*

Historiography on the other hand seems to exist on the highest level of inquiry, as well as of accounting, recounting, and recording. To wit, "the writing of history based on the critical examination of sources, the selection of details from the authentic materials, and the synthesis of these details into a narrative that will stand the test of critical methods." Thus one of my lexicons assures me, given ideal conditions or availability particularly of sources, if abundant. Often they are not abundant when dealing with events and persons of antiquity, whether of the Far East (China, India, Japan, etc.) or of the Far West (ancient Mesopotamia, Egypt, and the Graeco-Roman world of the Mediterranean Sea). Despite the patient copying and labors of scribes and scholars, many sources have disappeared because of destruction or attrition.

To turn to a modern example of an indirect history, let us mention Cyril W. Beaumont's *Complete Book of Ballets* (first published by Putnam, London, 1937), but as something more than what the subtitle indicates, *A Guide to the Principal Ballets of the Nineteenth and Twentieth Centuries.* Or as the author himself reminds us in his original preface, dated October 1937, "Read as a whole . . . [it also becomes] indirectly, an informal history of the ballet of that period." It remains, nonetheless, genuine history but narrated in a refreshingly different manner. Especially in the critical reactions in the contemporary press, sources for new productions remain relatively abundant, as compared to sources for Graeco-Roman history, where much material simply did not survive either due to the depredations of time or due to the vicissitudes of human existence. Although the latter seems rather obvious, such physical conditions deserve reiteration and emphasis.

On the other hand, vis-à-vis such informal but still genuine history, we have the recent multi-volume history of California by Kevin Starr, which we would regard as authentic historiography. Competent and informed critics have recognized this history for what it is, a truly remarkable if not superlative achievement. Very well and sensitively written, no less than judiciously balanced and even-handed, it does justice to the subject of California as the most populated state in the U.S. (c. 40 million people). The state well deserves a multi-volume history—such as Kevin Starr's magnum opus. His death on 15 January 2017 took from us not just an excellent historian but a true historiographer, a generous and humane individual as well as a rare genius in his particular niche or genre.

Kevin Starr was born in 1940, the year before the United States' entry into World War II began with the bombing of Pearl Harbor on 7 December 1941. Interestingly enough, he was born in the same year as Jack Foley of Oakland, the doyen of poets and writers in the San Francisco Bay Area, who for many long years has done more to encourage the literary arts in Northern California than anyone else. He has done this not only by the many poetry series that he has sponsored in the East Bay but above all by his outstanding half-hour radio program on KPFA (Berkeley), *Cover to Cover,* reaching the Bay Area overall, around it, and beyond.

Besides writing his own historical books on the poetry of the Bay Area from the mid-1900s onward, Jack Foley has featured an enormous variety of poets and writers on his program. He has thus amassed a huge collection of radio scripts and recordings, which in its entirety makes up an enormous historical archive, a kind of unofficial history just as it is. In a strict sense both Foley and Starr individually rank as historians, Jack somewhat informally and Starr quite formally. An unusual generosity of spirit has animated both individuals, otherwise existing in their own separate but interrelated spheres.

As emanating from both of these gentlemen, this generosity of spirit has benefited many relatively obscure literary figures, including the present author. In the case of Jack Foley, I owe an enormous debt of gratitude. To Kevin Starr my debt ranks as only a little bit less, albeit completely private, as well as undivulged until now. First, I should mention that Kevin Starr possessed a full fund of information and insight concerning Californian art, poetry, literature, and so forth, in addition to his grasp of political events and figures past and present. I believe that Jerry Brown, the current governor of California, had Starr as a professor at Loyola University in San Francisco, and thus had very good reasons to appoint him for a while as State Librarian (in Sacramento), a position that Starr abundantly deserved.

As one instance of Starr's magnanimity, I cite the following example from my own experience. Perceiving Kevin's especial interest in Californian literature, I sent him a signed copy of my own informal and modest literary history, *The Golden State Phantasticks: The California Romantics and Related Subjects* (Hippocampus Press, 2012), a hodgepodge chiefly concerned with Ambrose Bierce, George Sterling, Clark Ashton Smith, Nora May French (for whose work Starr nourished a predilection), and other associated figures.

Supremely well positioned to know the ins and outs of the subject of Californian Romanticism, Starr after due examination of my volume responded quite kindly (from his apartment on Franklin Street in San Francisco) by calling it "superb," an opinion that floored me at the time. For a relatively esoteric writer such as myself who has wisely never aspired to any kind of bestsellerdom, my real payment for my own books takes its form in such recognition as only a Kevin Starr can bestow. A most encouraging encomium, indeed!! That alone repaid me for writing the essays and then gathering them into the volume they became. (I should add that I have certainly received payment for the books that I have produced, however minimal it may be.) I remain deeply grateful to Kevin for his elevated opinion, however (perhaps) undeserved.

Overall I sent him four of my titles whether edited or authored by myself: *The Golden State Phantasticks; Gaspard de la Nuit* (translated from the French of Aloysius Bertrand [Black Coat Press, 2014]—this won the approbation of Judd Hubert, my favorite professor of French at U.C.L.A.); *The Outer Gate: The Collected Poems of Nora May French* (Hippocampus Press, 2009); and *The Atlantis Fragments* (Hippocampus Press, 2008), an omnibus volume featuring my collected poems. To all these titles dear Kevin responded cordially.

His generous reception of them all still raises up my spirits during the present winter of 2016-17.

As another example of a magnum opus (like Starr's multi-volume history of California) conceived and executed on a major scale and in considerable detail—albeit not yet published—I should cite what I could call the backstory for a major portion of Beaumont's *Complete Book of Ballets*. This considerable portion involves some half-dozen major balletmasters and not quite three dozen major ballets of the 1840s, the 1850s, and 1860s. This is my own story or history of the life and career of the Italian composer Cesare Pugni (1802-1870), who wrote music to order for many productions major and minor of the mid-1800s. Because of this composer's prominence, if not omnipresence, in the ballet theatre of his time (say, 1820-70), the history of his life and career overall becomes unavoidably the history of the ballet theatre of his period.

Highly rated in general during most of his life and career, Pugni and his music after his death became very poorly regarded. How could such a radical change of opinion have occurred? Apart from gaining access to the major source materials (mostly European, including Italian, British, French, German, and Russian), my main task consisted of investigating how this radical change of response, or opinion, happened to come about, no less than the aftermath to his life and career following Pugni's death, in the form of many further productions occurring in the Tsarist ballet theatre from 1870 on into the first two decades of the 1900s, that is, up to the two Russian Revolutions of 1917, February and October.

Researched and written in the spirit of an unobtrusive detective story, this magnum opus has as its full title the following: *The Case of the Light Fantastic Toe: The Romantic Ballet and Signor Maestro Cesare Pugni, as Well as Their Survival by Means of Tsarist Russia (A Chronicle and Source Book)*. Compiling and composing this opus provided me with my immediate experience of what is involved in researching and writing a major history. The research for it began in the 1950s and continued off and on until I began the actual writing in the late 1970s. It took me from late 1980 to late 2000 to achieve the typed manuscript, which then reduced itself in print from c. 5000 pages to c. 3000 pages. To do justice to the subject with all its ramifications (the Romantic Ballet and what came after it), quite apart from Pugni himself, I ended up writing an opus that in its depth and range still seems to myself (all proportions guarded) equivalent to *The Decline and Fall of the Roman Empire* by Edward Gibbon! So much more than just music is involved here.

Since its first real development as the splendiferous *ballet de cour* under Louis XIV, ballet remains an extraordinary *performing* art, whether in the form of dance drama or abstract ballet so called. As a collaborative art it implicates first the dancers, then the movement on the stage, the story or drama if any (whether narrated through dance or action scene), the sets and costumes (however defined), the music as brought to life by the conductor via some highly trained musicians, the lighting, and so forth. The music has become increasingly important since the late 1800s and early 1900s. Although an apparently positive development, it has had negative consequences as well.

Ever since the revolution or evolution effected by the Neo-Romantic Ballets Russes masterminded by Diaghilev, critics and audiences have unrealistically made too much depend on the musical element or component in and of itself. Inasmuch as any choreographer can devise any choreography to any music (whether intended for that purpose or not—sometimes it works well, sometimes not), and inasmuch as any dancers in the theatre or elsewhere can move to any music *or can move without it* (but only after careful and intensive preparation)—as proven absolutely by *La Création* as conceived and rehearsed by David Lichine (thus performed without music or metronome)—this overdependence on music by critics and audiences appears curiously misplaced. Certainly the earlier composers of music for ballet should not bear the aesthetic responsibility for later artistic revolutions that they could not have even imagined! The plight of poor Cesare Pugni remains a case in point. But let us move onward to other historical considerations.

We shall return to history here and there in some of our other essays, but for the time being let us close with these basic remarks that have no need to be original. Without inscriptions, without writing and written accounts, without printing and printed books, above all without history or any other mode of recording our thoughts and our actions, the human species has no real memory over the long term.

Old versus New

That *versus* above should really be *vis-à-vis*. No violent opposition or conflict intended or wanted. It was difficult to decide on a title for this essay relative to the various arts under discussion. I could have chosen "Traditional versus Nontraditional," as in poetry, but almost as much in the other arts that we are discussing in this monograph: "Abstract versus Representational" (relative to painting or sculpture), or "Conventional or Nonconventional," and so forth. But none of these quite capture the resonance of definition or meaning that I intend. Thus this "Old versus New" is just a *pis aller,* an expedient title in lieu of anything else.

First, let me declare my own principles as an artist in words, but sympathetic to the technical problems in the other arts and empathetic to the artists themselves. Whether one creates within the established norms and forms of a given art—to do that well is no small achievement, as anyone has discovered who has tried!—or whether one divagates from past examples in utter sincerity and skill—this often takes considerable determination and courage, and it is not always a conscious decision, but rather an irresistible compulsion to go against the grain, to do what the artist feels he must accomplish—the critic or spectator must applaud the given artist and the given result for the artist's individual bravery. If the resultant object of art does not please, then that is too bad, but all has occurred in an honest and straightforward manner, and otherwise only time will decide the matter.

As M. R. James has expressed it, if the intended audience is *not* pleased, it is a waste of time to try to tell them that they should be gratified. One remembers the opposition (or less than appreciation) that greeted such painters as Jackson Pollock or Mark Rothko. Time, however, has validated their courage and their art. Their paintings possess, or so it seems, an expressionistic force, if not angst, unique to our modern times. How tastes and perceptions have changed since the 1950s and the 1960s!

It is likewise difficult to assess abstract sculpture, except perhaps superficially, that is, as design, a stance that most critics disdain or decry; but sometimes initially it may turn out as the only one the spectator, or art-lover, can use, at least to perceive clearly the object, or the given style of the sculptured artifact. Whereas abstract can function in dance, painting, or sculpture—in any of the performance or graphic arts—it does not function very well in the written or printed medium, or as presented in literal recital, an obvious understatement.

In opera or oratorio, abstraction does not work well, or cannot do so. An opera needs a story, an anecdote, an episode, or a situation, to develop and present in some logical sequence however subtle or indirect. An opera, or an oratorio, needs a text especially created. Yet the best operas often remain those of the 1800s, especially the melodious and mellifluous Italian operas with their crisp consonants and open vowels. Moreover, these operas flatter the well-trained voice, and they do not always need those empty virtuoso pieces, a soprano in conjunction with a flute, serving no dramatic purpose. In dance and in ballet especially, such modern ballet-masters as G. Balanchine, F. Ashton, and J. Robbins, along with many others, have proven over and over again that abstract pieces, as regulated by nonballetic music, that is, by concert-hall music, can function magnificently, if not triumphantly. Yet we should not underappreciate the added resonance imparted by a story, a plot, a narrative artfully adapted to the medium of dance and action.

On the other hand, we might seriously doubt that abstraction would work well, or could exist, in a printed medium, even in a genre like tragedy or comedy, that is, in a spoken performance art. It could too easily turn into nonsense. I know of no examples of abstract speech in poetry or drama. It would simply appear incomprehensible, rather like baby talk lacking articulated and understandable words. Even examples of nonsense language tend to make sense, or the audience will insist on making or finding some kind of meaning.

Even poetry, modern and avant-garde material, whether in free verse and/or free form, makes some kind of sense willy-nilly, even if the reader must often puzzle it out. Otherwise, during a reading or recital, how long would an audience sit still during a presentation that might appear cast in pure gibberish? Once creators or artists push any language into total freedom, it becomes perforce unintelligible, unless people learn how to understand extended emotion-fraught ululations! Or for that matter, if a Shakespeare play could be performed in such a manner that the audience could not understand the words at all, how long would they sit still without eventually leaving, and asking for a refund of their tickets?

Another problem inheres relative to a popular art form as performed in a public milieu before a general audience, or relative to something comparatively esoteric presented before a specialized audience. In the first case we speak of movies; in the second case we speak of ballet. Once upon a time, during the 1930s, 1940s, then lessening in the 1950s, an enormous and respectful audience existed for the big feature films made in the Hollywood as well as in the European sound stages, many of them intelligently scripted, acted, and produced, often with creative flair, especially as emanating from the art direction, often dominated by skilled men of genius, not to mention apt and brilliant music produced by composers of genius usually working under pressure.

Although ballet as theatrical dance has now become much more popular than ever before (*The Red Shoes* in the mid-1900s had much to do with this increased popularity), such was not always the case in former times, as is obvious. Cyril W. Beaumont expresses this with a certain reserved poignancy in the preface to the first edition of his *Complete Book of Ballets*. "One of the most surprising events in the theatrical world during recent years has been the extraordinary and ever-increasing popularity of ballet. This art, which for many years relied for its support on a special public, is now enjoyed by audiences drawn from all classes."

Since the late 1930s, of course, that special audience has grown enormously with many regional ballet companies throughout the U.S. and the English-speaking world overall, no less than in Europe and the Far East, where they also have their own indigenous dance traditions, as in India, where the performing aesthetic principally falls on the arms as the expressive medium rather than on the legs as in the West, or the "Far West."

The important factor here in all these arts inheres in the freedom of the artist to experiment and innovate, even if only to validate or revalidate the older forms and norms, as sometimes happens. The older forms and norms can still function well when conscientiously practiced by skilled and gifted creative people. The conventional, or the traditional, and the unconventional, or the nontraditional, have always coexisted, whether overtly or clandestinely, often even harmoniously.

We have mentioned, relative to poetry, the existence of what might seem "pure gibberish" (by which we mean more than just foolish or voluble speech, but something totally unintelligible and meaningless), as well as "extended emotion-fraught ululations." Both forms of expression exist, especially the latter, strange to relate, and we are not referring to feral animals. Years agone, during my first extended sojourn in England (Winter 1971-72 to Spring 1972), my great and good friend Ian Law (since deceased) had thoughtfully arranged a meeting between me and a friend of his, a nontraditional British poet, Bob Cobbing, quite a pleasant gentleman and an enjoyable companion. We had a very good and profitable visit, even if we came at poetry from two different angles, myself as an innovative traditionalist, and Bob as a then very modern poet who had nonetheless passed through an earlier phase as a traditionalist. He thoroughly knew poetry ancient and modern, that is, in English, whether traditional or nontraditional.

Ian had already introduced him to my own poetry, my first collection, via his own copy of the First Series of *Songs and Sonnets Atlantean* (Arkham House, 1971), still my own favorite collection in certain respects, and certainly not juvenilia, as Bob had recognized at once, bless him!—given that I had created it during 1961-71, starting it when I was twenty-seven and completing it when I was thirty-seven. Then it appeared that same year when I turned thirty-seven. As is customary among poets, we read or recited a few of our own poems to each other with mutual and marked appreciation. Cobbing's own characteristic material seemed pretty deep to me and eminently worth experiencing. He had no copies of his own books on hand, but later I sent him a signed copy of my own First Series.

Then a major change of repertoire on his part. Bob played for me a tape of his most original stuff, some sort of a vocalization but without vocables. It seemed low-key (Bob had an agreeable masculine voice), and although it was not feral howling or wailing at full blast, as the term ululation might indicate, the only term that adequately describes it is ululation, albeit of a comparatively restrained intensity. One could possibly describe it as the music of the spoken or speaking voice, but not musical in the ordinary sense. Bob asked me what I thought of it, and he waited for my reply. Somewhat embarrassed, I tried to formulate an intelligent response. I stated that I thought it quite original, but I had no idea what it expressed. He nodded his head, smiled, and thanked me for my honesty.

Even though Bob had given readings of his own regular modern poetry (free verse and free form but still shaped into coherent phrases and statements), in what venue could he give a reading or recital of such novel material, I asked him. He had performed, or had played a tape of, this low-key ululation (just a few pieces), and the audience had responded politely, but seemed mystified. With rueful wisdom he smiled when he stated that the "academy," meaning colleges and universities, would not touch it for love nor money when he had sent them a copy of his best or better tapes featuring these idiosyncratic ululations. While innovation and originality do possess real significance, regular words in regular presentation bear more meaning than an unknown style of vocalization, alas!

Still, I reassured him how gratified my listening to this original material had made me, something vocal that pushed beyond mere language. I have never heard anything like it since that visit with Bob Cobbing in the winter of 1971-72.

Poetry and Poetry Again

Anyone reading my earlier essay on my own poetry, "A Defense and Illustration of One Poetic Method" (1976)—and anyone conversant with French and English Renaissance poetry—would recognize at once the deliberate reminiscence, in terms of the title, of the celebrated treatise *La Défense et Illustration de la langue française* (1549). In this remarkable opus the poet-author Joachim du Bellay (1522-1560) draws upon Greek, Latin, and Italian poetry in order to insist that the then modern poets could just as capably create a great modern poetry (in a modern vernacular, and French in his case) equal in value, meaning, and emotional resonance to the poetry of Graeco-Roman antiquity and that of the ongoing Italian Renaissance, the original one, whose example was already inspiring poetry in other countries and other languages, not to mention the other arts as well.

A substantial school of French poets had already come to exist in and around Lyon in southern France, but du Bellay's treatise served to form the even more remarkable group known as *la Pléiade,* and to inspire some of their greatest poets, du Bellay himself, Pierre de Ronsard, Remy Belleau, Jean-Antoine de Baïf, Fontus de Tyard, and so forth. Moreover, du Bellay's opus not only launched the Pléiade itself, but it exerted a similar influence just as great on the early poets of the English Renaissance, especially Wyatt and Surrey, the early Spenser, Sir Philip Sidney, and others, mostly prior to the Elizabethan and Jacobean dramatists, beginning with Christopher Marlowe and William Shakespeare.

The European Renaissance in literature came late to England, and moreover as that rebirth's last major development.

Most educated people in the United Kingdom read, spoke, and understood both written and spoken French, something that perforce went back to the Norman Conquest of 1066 and its immediate aftermath, when the very long process began that led to modern English. We could regard Chaucer's English in one sense as the earliest of early modern English, so different is it from Old English and Anglo-Norman.

My own use of the phrase "Defense and Illustration," while somewhat ironic, I meant in utter sincerity. Only I was arguing in reverse, treating the Elizabethan literary efflorescence in the same way as the Renaissance poets perceived Graeco-Roman literature. Faced with the bewildering and confusing chaos of poetry traditional and nontraditional in the late 1950s and early 1960s, I could not have begun creating poetry myself had I not discovered for myself Edmund Spenser's epic-romance-allegory *The Faerie Queene,* as urged to do so by three special friends, William Farmer of Auburn (California), and Fritz and Jonquil Leiber of Santa Monica and Pacific Palisades. Through that initial experience of reading and studying Spenser's epic (March through June of 1960) my own muse took flight, slowly and carefully. However, Spenser saved me from futile experimentation in modes utterly foreign to myself and to my then acquired knowledge.

Not only did Spenser save me from fruitless wandering, but he steered me to the forms and norms of the past, particularly of the Spenserian epoch, 1579–99. As I was completing my initial immersion in *The Faerie Queene,* I also perused *The Shepheardes Calender,* and I could perceive at once how that monumental achievement (1579) led irrevocably to the great epic. (That earlier opus has irresistible bits and pieces of sublime poetry.) I also discovered my own forms as adapted from *The Faerie Queene* in direct order, something quite comforting but utterly unanticipated! Surprises happen even for scholars, presumably steady and omniscient. Ha!

Faced especially with the obtuseness and chaos of much nontraditional modern poetry, I argued by my own example that a modern poet could revive, and work within, selected examples of the older forms and norms for his own purposes, even if avoiding purposed archaisms and forbidden poetic language. Even if it took me ten years, I achieved my goal by means of a mind-set not just from Spenser but from certain French poets of the Renaissance (mostly the 1500s), from Clément Marot to Agrippa d'Aubigné, as well as of the nineteenth century, the French Parnassians above all. What poets like Walt Whitman of the later 1800s, and Ezra Pound and T. S. Eliot of the early 1900s accomplished for themselves is all very well and good, but their example and poetry served no purpose for what I wanted to do. However, to achieve what I wanted to do required an extended period of time, a decade or so.

Using meter and rime, even if of the simplest kind, demands discipline, hard work, genuine soul-searching, and often at times endless fussing with given lines and phrases. On many occasions the poet must go through dozens of variations before finding that what he intuits is what he wants, especially in the art of translation. For example, certain lines and phrases in "L'Oubli" (Oblivion) by José-Maria de Heredia, no less than "La Beauté" (Beauty) by C. P. Baudelaire, made me go through 100 variations before I discovered the versions that finally satisfied my own taste and my own knowledge of both French and English. No burning poetic impetus must force the translator-poet to betray the poem and its own original inspiration by sloppy or incomplete workmanship. The same stricture applies even more forcibly to the poet's own original creations.

Even if I had read some of these French poets in class (college or university), I mostly experienced them in depth, and those in English, outside the academy. I often consulted with selected academic figures, teachers, and professors, some of whom became casual friends, and others close friends, the latter still in that category, except where deceased. All this discussion is by way of introduction to the subject of poetry in its widest sense. All this brings us to the chief issue concerning poetry. To wit, whether in antiquity or modernity, what is it that makes poetry so great? We need to ask this question because many people today who speak American English do not understand the primacy of poetry throughout the ages and for most human societies, whether Far Eastern or Far Western.

This cultural primacy of poetry stems from its acknowledged importance as the sum total of all the arts, especially in antiquity and in the European Renaissance from start to finish.

People thought that poetry contained painting and sculpture as embodied in the imagery of whatever type; music as projected through the meter and other means of verbal music (meter in Greek and Latin poetry is far more complicated and involved, never mind the necessity of declensions and conjugations); and finally, and above all else, language itself and the ability to use it to speak, to communicate, and to record notable events, as in history and historiography. In addition, and not at all incidentally, it conferred the capacity to compose things that are purely fictional, purposely created entities and places that could not exist otherwise than in the imagination, only in the otherworldly, known collectively as Otherwhere.

Where did all that put me then as a beginning poet-author in the early 1960s? I did not begin publishing my own scholarly essays until 1963. These I wrote for the most part on behalf of Clark Ashton Smith, to address the lack of critical comment of any real substance on him and his writings, that is, since the earlier part of his life and career, the 1910s and 1920s. However, other issues inevitably became involved.

I repeat my question: where then did all that put me as a beginning poet-author in the early 1960s? Apart from papers written for academic classes (high school and college), I had written nothing or very little. I had composed a dozen or so poems in adolescence (as published in a little newspaper put out by my brother and myself), attempts at traditional verse—pure and inept juvenilia—not worth collecting or publishing again. Thus at twenty-seven I began writing poetry more or less as tabula rasa indeed, or smoothed or erased tablet, but nevertheless with a head stuffed with all manner of lore and learning and knowledge, not excluding any amount of curious and esoteric odds and ends, as picked up all through my schooling, my military obligation, and especially my reading on my own in an unending succession of libraries public and private. I was also full of idiosyncratic prejudices and preferences in the arts but not in everyday life. Early in our shared existence our mother warned my brother and me against racial prejudice of any type, particularly against so-called black people. We picked out friends by affinity, and not by skin color.

Coming from eight years or more in French language and literature, and rediscovering English via *The Faerie Queene,* I had a definite predilection for employing the alexandrine, the classic line in traditional French prosody, not to mention Spenser's use of it at the end of the Spenserian stanza that he created for his nonpareil epic. I knew from the start that I would compose poetry in some traditional form, relatively brief, but featuring rime and meter, most likely iambic; and I knew by prior study and memorization of much poetry in English (and French) that I would encounter hard work and considerable difficulty. Imagine my surprise when my first experiment came out as the "Avalonessys" that begins what became the First Series of *Songs and Sonnets Atlantean.* I showed it to a few poetry-savvy friends, who pronounced upon it with favor. Thus encouraged, I continued. The poem itself remains a classic Italian, or Petrarchan, sonnet but cast in alexandrines, rhyming ABBA ABBA (octet) CDE CDE (sestet).

Then I ran into another problem. If I purposed to write a number of sonnets, then I had to choose consciously what particular type I would employ: the standard, Petrarchan, or regular sonnet with the rime scheme as laid out above; the English, or Elizabethan, sonnet consisting of three quatrains and a couplet: ABAB CDCD EFEF GG; then the Spenserian sonnet, also with three quatrains and a couplet but with the quatrains interlinked by rime: ABAB BCBC CDCD EE. At once I had noticed that the sonnet's first nine lines duplicated the arrangement and rime-scheme in the Spenserian stanza.

After "Avalonessys" the second selection ultimately became a poem in prose, one of my first conscious attempts at writing in such an eminently French genre. I had made a special study of the genre during my final years at U.C.L.A., with special emphasis on *Gaspard de la Nuit,* the collection of prose ballads by Aloysius Bertrand (1842), which has many affinities in style and content with *Les Trophées* by José-Maria de Heredia (1893). But it was the third selection in this first collection of my own that threw me back on my resources and initiative, the sonnet "Atlantis," which I cast as a Spenserian sonnet only half-consciously, merely as an experiment to witness what would emerge. I created the first nine lines as a Spenserian stanza, lengthening the ninth line into an alexandrine. And then the next three lines insisted on becoming fourteeners and broke away from the first nine lines as a separate unit, that is, as a tercet but linked by rime to the preceding; and the final couplet likewise insisted on becoming fourteeners as well.

So what had I wrought inadvertently, without any preconception to do so? I had created an interesting and viable variation of the Spenserian sonnet, which I later correctly termed the Spenserian stanza-sonnet, usually consisting of a Spenserian stanza, a tercet, and a couplet, the last five lines generally longer, that is, as alexandrines or fourteeners. Later, as time went one, I would use both the regular Spenserian sonnet and my own variant of it, but increasingly the latter, to demonstrate its validity as well as its potential for multifarious applications in subject matter.

Voilà, I had created my very own form; but as I soon discovered, to use it well took much time and care. Off and on I spent three years on the third selection "Atlantis" alone before I had it as I wanted it, as I thought that it should shape up. After this major prosodic innovation, I also discovered the possibility of using a single Spenserian stanza in and of itself as a viable but very short form for lyrical expression. And in one morceau, "Your Mouth of Pomegranate," I discovered or created a new form of blank verse, but cast or developed in alexandrines, as more or less iambic hexameters (that is, in English). Although the alexandrine is the standard line in French classic poetry (as already stated), it is comparatively rare in English. However, this further prosodic innovation, alexandrine blank verse (whatever meter it might employ), I myself would not feature on any great scale until the Second and Third Series, and in only a few narratives, of course, in verse.

By creating a new sonnet form, by reviving a much shorter lyric form, and by creating a new kind of blank verse, I had promised or guaranteed myself a certain prosodic originality. All I needed to do (as if that were not enough), was to work assiduously, to work very long and hard, with patience and acumen, and voilà, I might come up with a viable corpus of original poetry. The first two series took me ten years each to complete, and the third one only three. My last two collections, each only about 100 pages (MS. or published), have each required some two years. Yes, a lot of arduous work, but more than worth it in terms of the printed books.

In my earlier essay on "One Poetic Method," I could have saved myself and the reader much tedious bother by simply dismissing Mark Purcell's comments (whether overtly negative or not), and then by declaring my own critical stance (rather different from his), quite apart from the fact of authorship, the latter belonging to me in the case of *Songs and Sonnets Atlantean.* Like Ashton Smith's own stance, my position remains "old-fashioned and aesthetic." Like the English Romantics (e.g., Coleridge, Wordsworth, Shelley, Keats, Beddoes, etc.), Ashton Smith and I continue to stay committed to Beauty in all seriousness, however unfashionable it might seem, at least superficially.

This amounts to much more than "pretty writing" (but there is nothing wrong with that). Can Purcell not distinguish between "the pretty" and "the beautiful"—the latter, that is, in a Platonic sense as formulated by Plotinus? Enough said! Technically, in spite of all that I derive personally as a poet from other poets (and what poet does not?), my work remains original, apart from reminiscence conscious or unconscious. As forthrightly stated on the dedication page of the First Series of *Songs and Sonnets Atlantean,* quoting from dear and clairvoyant Phil Ochs: "Ah but in such an ugly time the true protest is beauty."

About the same time as I was creating my first mature poetry (from age twenty-seven to age thirty-seven), and as I was responding to Spenser's two chief works (*The Faerie Queene* and *Shepheardes Calender*)—this was when I was creating the earlier "Avalonessys" and "Atlantis"—I also began my serious examination of the French Parnassian poets, the second generation of the French Romantics, above all Leconte de Lisle (as unequivocally great as Baudelaire and certainly greater than Rimbaud). He teaches many valuable lessons, not the least of which is the avoidance of certain aspects of the intimately personal, especially the worst kinds of humanistic slop and garbage. In his cosmic perspective an extraordinary strength and clear-headedness inhere. We thank him for his pioneering viewpoint, which anticipates the even stronger cosmic-astronomic-mindedness that we find so powerfully delineated or presented in Lovecraft, Ashton Smith, and Robert E. Howard, not to forget George Sterling.

But, because of simple proximity and circumstance, we rediscovered his most extraordinary disciple, José-Maria de Heredia, whose one extraordinary collection, *Les Trophées* (1893), sums up the French Parnassian stance in an especially compact, concise, and resplendent manner. That book, in just a bit less than 120 sonnets, provides a series of amazing and gorgeous adventures, mostly expert historical recapitulation but brilliantly manifested. Thus, beyond George Sterling and Ashton Smith, I discovered, or rediscovered, sources of the cosmic-astronomic that preceded them. Smith at least knew to some degree the *oeuvre* of Leconte de Lisle and Heredia even before he learned French on his own during the first half of the 1920s. However, following that learning experience, Smith proceeded to deepen his knowledge and examination of the two chief French Parnassians, among many other poets non-Parnassian.

About the same time (the early 1960s) that I began studying and memorizing from the works of Leconte de Lisle and Heredia, I also began a serious and fruitful examination of what had already become one of my favorite books in any language, the one, the only, the unique *Gaspard de la Nuit* (1842) by Aloysius Bertrand, to observe more closely how he had managed to create a new genre, the *poème en prose,* and to create substantial examples in this his new category of literature. (Not for nothing did Baudelaire love this exquisite volume.) Thus, as I had already launched myself on the long-term adventure of *Songs and Sonnets Atlantean,* I had Bertrand and Heredia as my literary companions, only a little bit less constant than Edmund Spenser and Ashton Smith.

As a kind of codicil I should add here, at the end of this my second major essay concerning my own poetry, a bit more about the reaction to my own "Parnassian" stance. Ashton Smith's epochal collection *Ebony and Crystal,* as published by Smith himself in December of 1922, had already exerted on me a far greater influence (in terms of pure Parnassianism quite a bit in advance of the French Parnassians themselves) than either Bertrand or Leconte de Lisle. This especial influence from C.A.S. waxed at its most powerful for me during the 1950s and early 1960s. However, thanks to Sterling and his first collection, *The Testimony of the Suns* (1903), Ashton Smith emphasized the cosmic, or the cosmic-astronomic, element far more forcibly than what appears among the French Parnassians. Of course, I had already noticed this element in depth as purveyed in Smith's parables in prose, his short stories, as first published in *Weird Tales* and *Wonder Stories* in the 1930s, and then gathered in book form during the 1940s by Arkham House.

Sometime after I moved in with Rah Hoffman (with whom I resided from Summer 1998 until his death in Winter 2012-13), I read an obituary in the *Los Angeles Times* concerning the death of Renée Hubert at her home in Newport Beach, the spouse of my single favorite French professor at U.C.L.A, Judd Hubert, during my regular years of attendance there (1956-60). He had also become a friend to me, a mere undergraduate, which says much about his kindness and humanity. Via the obituary I discovered that he was still alive and residing at the family home in Newport Beach. I located his telephone number and his mailing address, and wrote him a note in English. He responded in English and addressed me at the start of his letter as "Dear Friend." We soon switched to French in our letters.

Sometime not long after that, I sent him a signed copy of the First Series of *Songs and Sonnets Atlantean.* After reading and assimilating it, Judd acknowledged it with thanks and warm appreciation, addressing me as "Mon cher Parnassien." Judd knew at least French, German, and English literature (that is, in those languages) in depth. And his use of "Parnassian" in addressing me made me realize at once that he grasped my poetry, and that he thus let me know that he rated the book quite highly, given the impeccable (technical) standards of the French Parnassians, whatever else one might think of their *oeuvre.*

That my poetry used meter and rime and employed several traditional forms, even if in an innovative manner—that the book was patently Old School in one sense—made no difference to him and did not prejudice him against my work, but produced just the opposite effect. I could have received no greater accolade, even if given more implicitly than overtly, and even if he did include some direct words of praise in his letter. When the first deluxe edition of my collected poems came out in 2008 *as The Atlantis Fragments,* I mailed him a signed copy. Earlier, with the First Series, like most literature-savvy people, he especially enjoyed the mock-scholarly apparatus of "Introduction" and "Notes" by Dr. Ibid M. Andor, with both the subtle humor and the sense of serious play. Some little time after his receipt of the omnibus volume, he wrote me a note of acknowledgment and warm appreciation, referring to the poetry omnibus as "your great book."

This high praise did not give me a big head, it did not make me feel conceited, but rather it endowed me with a feeling of the most profound satisfaction. His approval meant more to me than anyone else's. Later he likewise approved of my translation of *Gaspard de la Nuit,* and he appreciated the depth of the research I had achieved to write the major essay on Bertrand that served as the introduction to that volume. Always in the company of my great and good friend, John D. Miller of Glendale—who drove us down to Newport Beach many times, bless him!—Judd, his daughter, John, and I spent many enjoyable visits together, invariably capping each visit by going out for a late afternoon or early evening meal at one of the excellent eateries with which that affluent region abounds. John in turn became a close and valued friend to Judd and his daughter. John and I attended, of course, Judd's ninetieth birthday party that daughter Candice, or Candi, put on for him at their home, a wonderful catered affair. She works as a California State Park ranger in San Diego County and looked after her father until his death.

Judd, a small compact man, enjoyed excellent health throughout his life, including his nineties, and his longevity amazed him as much as anyone else. We all thought and expected that he would reach the status of centenarian. Alas, during the winter of 2015-16 he developed pneumonia, and in spite of the best medical attention, including hospitalization, the medical people had him return to his home, where he passed on during the night of 24 January 2016. Although now gone from us just a little over a year, Judd Hubert remains to this day, for myself at least, one of the most extraordinary literary people whom I could have known. I miss him not just as my favorite French professor but above all as a great and very dear and eminently humane friend and a human being in the fullest sense.

I should add that a week before his death he did in fact reach the age of ninety-nine on his last birthday, Sunday, 17 January 2016. How our literary conversations come back to haunt me! Of course, Judd had considerable knowledge of the imaginative literature of Europe, and especially of France, from the Middle Ages through the Renaissance and on into the early modern period. I need only mention *Le Roman de la rose* by Guillaume de Lorris and Jean de Meung representing the High Middle Ages, the *L'Astrée* by Honoré d'Urfé and other enormously long romances in prose of the Renaissance, not to leave out the exquisite fairy tales of Charles Perrault and similar writers. Although he had not read much modern fantasy and science fiction, he did know of it. He also knew such modern fantasy films as *La Belle et la Bête* by Jean Cocteau, which he rightly considered a masterpiece. At the time we discussed it, while I attended U.C.L.A., I had not yet seen it—rather should I say, I had not *experienced* it—an oversight since rectified many times over!

In bits and pieces I introduced him to the poetry of George Sterling and Clark Ashton Smith, especially the latter's *Poems in Prose*

(1965); he seemed impressed. Judd studied the last-cited volume, and he knew the French poem in prose thoroughly, from Bertrand through Baudelaire and Rimbaud to Lautréamont. After handing the volume back to me (my own copy), he commented, comparing it with the examples in French, "They are very different." (Indeed they are! But I had already demonstrated that difference during an earlier visit, when I had recited "The Memnons of the Night" with as much strength and vocal dexterity as I could.) He grasped how, following in the immediate footsteps of Sterling, Smith, and Nora May French, I had continued and enriched the tradition(s) of the California Romantic poets. Because he knew quite well the work of the French Parnassians, he could perceive how my own poems in verse and prose, unlike the historical re-creations by Heredia in *Les Trophées,* had the advantage of the freedom, the wide-ranging outlook, implicit in modern fantasy and science fiction, as I had explained it to him. Judd, bless him, kept an open mind on into ninety-nine, up until his death! What a miracle!

Re-reading certain books on certain recurrently favorite subjects (I am speaking here of my own tastes and preferences, of course), I find myself intrigued again by José-Maria de Heredia and *Les Trophées* (1893) and Colin Wilson writing about music in *On Music* (1964, 1967). I first read the last-cited book in a paperback edition somewhere back in the 1970s, as I was urged to do so by Rah Hoffman. I found it, and still find it, a stimulating experience indeed. We shall discuss this book, but in brief, at the end of this essay. Of greater interest to me by far there remain Heredia and his condensed lyrics with epic overtones, very well characterized by his daughter Marie de Heredia, later Madame Henri de Régnier, who wrote under the name of Gérard d'Houville, as follows: "infranchissables," that is, insurmountable, or insuperable, referring to the 118 more or less perfect sonnets making up his one and only collection.

I am re-reading two relatively recent biographies of Heredia that I first read a decade or more back in time—*José-Maria de Heredia,* by Alvin Harms (Boston: Twayne, 1975), and *Heredia,* by W. N. Ince (London: Athlone Press, 1979)—both pioneering accounts of his life, career, and poetic achievement, at least in English; both exemplarily researched and written. Despite the cautious hedging so characteristic of the best academic writers, the reader still manages to learn much about Heredia and the period in which he lived. Like George Sterling, but in a very different way, he lived a fortunate and fulfilled existence. His life turned out as it did, not only because of his genius, but above all because of his comfortable financial situation both as a child and as an adult. Born on 22 November 1842, his wealthy-planter parents (then living in Cuba) raised him and their other children in a kind and considerate manner. But the main task of upbringing fell to his Norman-French mother after her husband unexpectedly died on 15 April 1849, when José was only seven years old. Later, when the son went to France for schooling there, a close friend of his family looked after him, and counseled him, in a quite parental manner—one Nicholas Fauvelle.

This re-reading has made me review and re-experience much of *Les Trophées*. How very different these not quite 120 magisterial sonnets remain from the earliest ones in the Italian of the Middle Ages!—concerned as they are by the given poet as revolving around some beautiful female, his love for her (unrequited or not), and the various ups and downs of mood and emotion instigated by the poet's varying perception of the belovèd. Early in his life, as a young adult, Heredia set himself the task to stage in his epico-lyrical sonnets the re-creation of strategic moments largely in European history and mythology from antiquity up to modern times, but not concerned with the latter in political terms (for which we give profound thanks). Under whatever other aegis he may have created, Heredia remained constant in his devotion to Nature, dream, and reverie, or daydream, as poetic inspiration.

Compared to Heredia's method of individual historical or mythological recreations, involving much research and then intentionally balanced reflection—looking at everything in an overall perspective with great care and judicious choice—my own method appears to me more intuitive and much easier in one sense. I am dealing with imaginary sites and events, certainly not all mythological, but handling them as if they had genuine physical or geographical reality, and as part of a larger background story, which imposes its own demands of continuity, no less than consistency. For a poet who has chosen to work with meter, rime, and stanza in whatever combination or layout, such a poet as myself, the chief problem inheres in the use of such a rime-poor language as English, and in the selection of the given form and its rime-scheme (if one exists in advance per tradition), rather like grafting what the poet has in mind to express onto a simple crossword-puzzle arrangement.

To return to, and finish this essay with, the always amazing and stimulating Colin Wilson, and in this case to do so with his "Brandy of the Damned" (the original title), indeed—*On Music,* or *Colin Wilson on Music.* My admiration for him and his work should not at all appear suspect. The two of us exist at the antipodes of each other. Whereas he lives in a realm of ideas for the most part (with a very large admixture of aesthetics but in a way different from myself), I live as much as possible in a realm of poetic imagery and aesthetics (but not without a few ideas, even if not emphasized or featured in some blatant manner). In this particular book Wilson is largely concerned with what sometimes is called "serious music," the great symphonic or operatic traditions (the operatic rather less) from the latter 1700s on through the latter 1900s, one of the most salient periods of musical evolution in the Western World that nobody of intelligence, also well informed, could refute! I grew up in New England with such music, but we called it "classical music," quite apart from the twentieth-century recapitulation of such musical history (that is, for the same period) as classical, Romantic, and modern.

For purposes of easy discussion, before we look at what Wilson has to say concerning music, let us divide music, serious or otherwise, into two main categories, even if music exists anywhere in any form at any particular time, not just in terms of the invaluable trained musicians who perform it. There is music for the concert hall, and there is music for the opera house, whether this involves heavy-duty serious music or light or light-hearted music, although the two types often intertwine in the same composition. French, Italian, and Spanish composers have largely written some of their best music for the opera house. German as well as other Northern and Central European composers have largely written for the concert hall as their chief venue, but this declaration does not in any way disparage or underestimate the composers of so-called light music, whether of singspiel, opéra-comique, zarzuela, Italian comic opera, or the operettas of Gilbert and Sullivan; or for that matter the American musical comedy.

Colin Wilson must rank as one of the most interesting critics or commentators on music whom I have myself read. It is just as well that he is not a trained musician, but rather one of the best *listeners* of music ever. Listening to serious music is an art. Had he been a trained musician, it would only have confused him in his clairvoyant stance or capacity as a paramount listener and assimilator of music. He does particularly well, if not superbly, concerning the great Austro-Germanic tradition of symphonic development from Haydn, Mozart, and Beethoven on through the main part of the 1800s, ending with Brahms, Wagner, Bruckner, and Mahler. He also deals very well with the so-called problem of modern music, including Stravinsky, Schoenberg, Webern, Bartok, Berg, Boulez, Hindemith, and so forth, some of whom have won acceptance into the pantheon of acknowledged masters, that is, as great composers.

Wilson writes perceptively and with appreciation on composers as distinct from each other as Frederick Delius, Alexander Scriabin, and Ernst Bloch, not to mention the considerable appeal and worth of jazz, whether Dixieland or progressive. He comments rather harshly on English music, no less than on American music, seemingly unimpressed by the vitality and genuine worth of American musical comedy, the closest that the U.S. has come to an indigenous form of opera. To me he seems rather dismissive of both the English and the American symphonists. Well might the Austro-Germanic tradition of symphonic music have impressed Wilson, and justifiably, but some of the non-Germanic composers, especially the Russians, have produced symphonic music just as eloquent and impressive.

However, let us not forget that, as we have stated earlier, we can find music all over our planet, that is, wherever humans exist, anywhere in any form at any time, whether in live performance or in recorded form, wherever anyone sings or hums or whistles; and not just in terms of the indispensable trained musicians, wherever extant in the Far Eastern or the Far Western world. Highly developed music of all types exists throughout the human world, whether North African, Middle Eastern, Indic (that is, of India herself), Chinese, Southeast Asian, and Indonesian: it is almost beyond counting. We regret that such a superb critic or commentator as Colin Wilson appears to be boxed exclusively into the Austro-Germanic symphonic tradition—that is, in terms of his deepest appreciation—or into any other purely European mode or practice of music.

Music and poetry have developed side by side since time immemorial, but the music of poetry is not quite the same thing. What music and poetry do often share in equal measure is the sense or the play of fantasy.

Perfect Form, Perfect Shape

Even if in the Western World we (as human beings mostly in urban areas) develop and mature surrounded by sculptures made out of all manner of material—often statues of celebrated people, no less than of non-human species, often found in public parks and plazas, as well as in cemeteries, and generally of a representational or traditional type—how often do we ponder the cause and effect of such sculptures as embodied in statues or groups of statues, or cast in metals like bronze, brass, and copper, or made real in wood or ceramic or porcelain?

Whether sculpted in stone in studios and/or cast in foundries, large-scale statues are labor-intensive and very expensive, the expense borne by wealthy individuals or from special campaigns for funds as contributions from among a wide assortment of people. All those predictable life-sized sculptures, for example, of renowned generals on horseback—whether the equine mounts are firmly standing on all four hooves, or are rearing up, secured only by the back hooves—cost a great deal of money.

Whether they finish up as conventional sculptures or not, the artist (highly trained over a long period of time) has had to expend much time, care, and art to accomplish that predictable appearance. Sometimes the sculptor does the job at least competently and professionally, but then at other times with unmistakable flair.

However, in each and every case it usually represents an extended period of time. It requires patience, considerable physical toil, and genuine vision.

As in poetry—traditional versus free verse and free form—thus in sculpture a similar dilemma confronts the artist on how to define free form and free shape, on how to define any new piece with any originality, on how to find patronage, thus veering away from the traditional or representational, even if the sculptors do stylize their work in some form or fashion. At any rate the sculptor-artist can achieve it, and has in fact achieved it.

The abstract work accomplished by Isamu Noguchi surely has form, as well as very well rendered and convincing shape. Nonetheless, much abstract sculpture still often retains representational elements, however minimal, however deployed. These elements give the imagination a solid hook from which to hang a variety of associations, or a prism from which to suggest other perspectives, whether for the artist or the onlooker in his role as basic spectator or highly evolved connoisseur.

More often than not, sculpture and architecture have combined to stunning effect, and superabundantly, throughout the world and throughout history east and west. We need allude only to the vast subcontinent of India, to southeast Asia (Angkor in Cambodia), or to selected locations in Polynesia, such as Pohnpei (Nan Madol), Kosrae (Leluh), and Easter Island, all these featuring spectacular examples. The Hindu temples with sculptures multifarious in India alone exist almost beyond counting!

Prodigious specimens survive from Ancient Mesopotamia (in particular, from Assyria and Babylonia), but what survives from Ancient Egypt literally beggars description, extending from more than 4,500 years, and so much of it on such a colossal scale that the student must witness it in person to believe it. The Egyptian sculptors gained universal respect and admiration as a group, and sometimes found employment elsewhere. The Achaemenian Persian Emperors used Egyptian sculptors at Persepolis with impressive results.

Even when not on a colossal scale, Egyptian sculpture can take rank on occasion as artistic artifacts only describable as exquisite. We cite here as a supreme example the ideal bust of Queen Nefertiti, chief wife to Amenhotep IV, or Akhenaten, that German archaeologists discovered among the ruins of Akhetaten, or Amarna. The Eighteenth Dynasty, to which these rulers belonged, ordinarily ruled from Waset, or Thebes, in Upper Egypt during the 1500s, 1400s, and 1300s B.C. Thutmose (Thoth-Moses), one of the sculptors for Akhenaten's court, created this bust among many other sculptures, and remains one of the few Egyptian sculptors whose name we happen to know, the chance result of archaeological investigation.

As for the Graeco-Roman world of antiquity, so many specimens have survived either in their original condition or in some reproduced form that they have come to seem almost commonplace.

This art, architecture, and sculpture laid the foundation for so much of our Western art in later periods as again to exist almost beyond counting. Even if we do know the names for some of the Greek sculptors, including Phidias, whose *floruit* occurred around 490–430 B.C., we do not necessarily know those for many or most of the sculptors who belonged to the school of artists that flourished at Aphrodisias in southwestern Asia Minor. For centuries their works circulated throughout the Mediterranean world and even beyond, as in the case of the British Isles. Thus we have many statues of Roman emperors done by Greek sculptors of the highest rank, including Hadrian and his favorite Antinous (in the case of the last named, at least as many as for any emperor).

Coming closer to our modern times, from the Renaissance onward, most art-savvy people know many of the sculptures of such universally acclaimed names as Michelangelo, Jean-Antoine Houdon, Antonio Canova, Frédéric-Auguste Bartholdi, and Auguste Rodin. Bartholdi it was who sculpted and then cast in copper the Statue of Liberty located in New York City harbor, given as a gift by France to the U.S. and unveiled in 1886. The sculptors of the Art Deco period of the 1920s and 1930s accomplished many exceptional pieces of suave and stylized conception as well as execution. We need only recall the many fine examples at Rockefeller Center in mid-Manhattan, some of it displaying an influence from Ancient Egyptian models.

Art Deco flowed imperceptibly into the later abstract sculpture of artists like Isamu Noguchi, the outstanding and quite original Japanese American sculptor. We mention his ethnicity simply to indicate that he possessed to the maximum degree the high sense of aesthetics characteristic of the Japanese wherever found, whether in Japan or in the U.S. This outstanding pioneer of perfectly realized abstract sculpture achieved a body of work that, for all its freedom and innovation, and obviously while not representational, is definitely not amorphous, but rather genuinely polymorphous. Noguchi and his body of work stand quite alone, but have proven beneficial and influential for many other masters of abstract sculpture.

Among the best-known sculptures done in our modern period, the colossal heads on Mount Rushmore (located in the Black Hills in western South Dakota) take rank for size with such prodigies of gigantic scope as the seated Pharaonic figures at Abu Simbel in the far south of modern Egypt. Sculpted by Gutzon Borglum and his son

Lincoln Borglum during 1927-39, and thus achieved under federal patronage, the carven heads, each 60 feet high, of four U.S. presidents—Washington, Jefferson, Lincoln, and Theodore Roosevelt—remain to this day some of the most extraordinary sculptures ever realized in hard stone. The difficulties and logistics of such travail almost literally defy belief. Truly fantasies or shapings in some of the hardest materials found on our planet!

As for myself, even if I do not know the subject of sculpture in any great range or depth, and even if I have not taken many courses in art and art history, I have known a small number of sculptors and their work. First, as reported in the essay on Jesse Allen's first mural, I recently came to know the painter and sculptor Lerey. As a painter he practices the pictorial art by helping Jesse with some of his paintings, that is, he fills in with corroborative and repetitive but necessary detail. As a sculptor on the hacienda he practices the art of sculpture in tropical woods by creating large medallions placed here and there on the hacienda (as at the front metal gate), or by making furniture with decorative motifs for some of the rooms in the main house, and in the art studio. Lerey's work in wooden sculpture is perfectly competent and professional, but unlike Jesse I admire Lerey's artistic or painterly skills far more, in particular his versatility. However, I have not seen or inspected his detached sculptures in wood, which might make me think more highly of him as a sculptor pure and simple.

The other sculptor whose work I know rather well is none other than Clark Ashton Smith, many of whose little sculptures I first came to inspect on my first visit with him at Pacific Grove in the summer of 1959. I have also examined "up close" one of his two larger sculptures, both made out of some hard stone. The larger one that I inspected is Ialdabaoth, per some accounts the idiot creator god. This piece measures 8 inches tall by $3\frac{1}{2}$ inches wide for the upper half and 4 inches wide at the bottom. For these two larger sculptures Ashton Smith used a hammer, or mallet, with a heavy chisel. All his other sculptures he made out of some soft material such as talc, which evidently hardens over time when exposed to the air. He could hold a typical small sculpture in one hand and work on it with the other hand while wielding a penknife. None of the sculptures are uniform, and they are idiosyncratic and individual to a high degree, generally outré figurines, many drawing upon his personal mythologies deriving from his fictional other worlds of Hyperborea, Poseidonis, Averoigne, and Zothique.

The other sculptors whose work I knew but as a child when living at Presidential Heights in New Bedford, Massachusetts, constituted a much humbler class of workers. These were the artisans who worked in one or more small workshops in the double cemetery at the top of the moderate slope or ridge on which sits the housing project, the slope that went east and west in length. These artisans, or artists (if you will), worked on the monuments for the burials to identify those whose bodies it was in the coffins interred in the burial plots or plats. The work they did was conventional and representational, whether in imagery or apropos of the incised letters, but perforce had to measure up to professional standards: the monuments involved tombstones, Christian crosses, and other features.

When traversing one or the other cemetery, and sometimes visiting the grave of some close relative (always on my mother's side, French or French-Canadian), I would stop off and talk briefly with one or more of the artisans, who generally would welcome me, but who would soon resume their regular work while I would wander back home. Of course, I never met any of the sculptors who created, or who had created, some of the fancier statues around town, especially downtown. My own favorite became, and remained, the harpooneer in the front of the rowboat that stood to the right of the old main library (that faced east) in downtown New Bedford just south of the City Hall. I believe man and boat were cast in iron and stood on a granite plinth with an upright piece of granite behind the harpooneer. On this upright extension from the plinth a large official plaque was affixed with raised printing on the metal of the plaque. The legend reads "A Dead Whale or a Stove Boat." That whales are overall relatively gentle creatures made the job of killing the individual cetaceans much easier than if they had been viciously aggressive!

Yet one rarely sees the whales themselves in fanciful depictions, despite their enormous contribution to the dominant species and their culture on the terrain of New England! In fact, apart from the often exquisite small-scale figurines often offered for sale at the various fantasy and science-fiction conventions, the avid spectator almost never finds anywhere any major group of whatever statuary could take shape apart from the ubiquitous and enchanting unicorn (whether equine or caprine), whenever the anthropocentric per se does not predominate. Unequivocally human beings are in love with themselves individually and collectively.

Atlantis

Translated from the Atlantean of Athallarion.

An alpha huge athwart the Ocean Sea,
The island continent Atlantis, old
In thrice-resplendent sovereign empery,
Uprose from deeps now deeper still. In gold.
And orichalch it pleased her to enfold
The pomp, the pride, of her imperial court;
Where Beauty flamed her flambeaux manifold,
And blazing Wealth maintained its foremost port,
Enshrined—O Empire's heart—in Empire's uttermost fort:

O fortress . . . pharos . . . archsublime acropolis of kings;
Where once the crown and trident swayed that pompous prideful court,
And Majesty in splendent state would muse splendid things. . . .

O Splendor sunk, alas! beyond recall, that once of yore
Her crown and trident's empire stretched from east to western
    shore. . . .

Alas! And now no more . . . For ever more. . . . Alas!

One Poetic Practice

One poetic practice? I might as well use the word belief or credo, rather than practice, and I have already used "One Poetic Method." But I shall settle for practice, meaning here a working method. How does one, how do I, negotiate creating a poem long or short? If it is an extended narrative in blank verse, that generally proves somewhat easier. But if it is brief and involves rime, or something like rime, that always turns out more challenging.

If in his working method José-Maria de Heredia surely had his travail cut out for him—and yes, he certainly did!—then I in my own manner of poetic labor face a different challenge when I create a much shorter poem, say, one of my own sonnets. I have already touched on this topic in my previous essay "Poetry and Poetry Again." Since I have already presented the problem cogently and coherently, I can do no better than to quote my own formulation.

> Compared to Heredia's method of individual historical or mythological recreations, involving much research and then intentionally balanced reflection—looking at everything in an overall perspective with great care and judicious choice—my own method appears to me to be more intuitive and possibly easier in one sense. I am dealing with imaginary sites and events, certainly not all mythological, but handling them as if they had genuine physical or geographical reality, and as part of a larger background story, which imposes its own demands of continuity, no less than consistency. For a poet who has chosen to work with meter, rime, and stanza in whatever combination or layout, that is, for such a poet as myself, the chief problem inheres in the use of such a rime-poor language as English, and in the selection of the given form and its rime-scheme (if one exists in advance per tradition), rather like grafting what the poet has in mind to express onto a simple crossword-puzzle arrangement. [Exactly!]

However created, with however much hard labor or travail, the result—especially if it results in something obviously successful in an artistic sense—can give unending satisfaction. This is true whether the finished product might be *Les Trophées* by José-Maria de Heredia or

Fungi from Yuggoth by H. P. Lovecraft. In the latter case the insights offered by the modern fantasy and science-fiction perspective open up infinite possibilities, cosmic, astronomic, macrocosmic, or microcosmic, taking a long and leisurely look at certain small details ripe with potential and significance for future development.

Development? Obviously I am not speaking here in terms popularized by Jules Verne, that is, inventing or developing new machines or appliances to make certain aspects of human life and industry easier and more convenient. Rather do I refer to some rich vein of potential creation in terms of future poetic development. Although they now have an unlimited canvas with free verse and free form, poets have not yet quite exhausted the possibilities of the traditional forms and norms, even if they should avoid certain clichés and hackneyed approaches. The clichés have evolved largely because of the rime-poor nature of English, American or British, which of course covers an enormous area linguistically and geographically.

The limited number of certain rime words has guaranteed a limited number of thought patterns to express certain emotions, and therefore a limited number of poetic phrases, thus leading to clichés, or variations of clichés. A traditional poet learns to avoid these formulations, or uses them with discretion, or not at all, unless for satire or irony. The nontraditional poets who employ free verse and free form can thus at least avoid those clichés occasioned or dictated by the limited number of certain rime words, not just obvious examples like *dove, love, above, of,* and *glove,* but less evident ones like *court, port,* and *fort.* The scarcity of certain rime words can certainly test the ingenuity and imagination of the dedicated poet working in traditional forms with rime and meter! And when halfway through a sonnet, nothing could be more discouraging for a poet when stuck or stymied by the lack of a suitable rime word, even if he has meditated the rime scheme in advance.

However, the resourceful poet develops techniques or strategies to deal with problems like these. Let us take the ensample (neat variant of example) of the three basic long "oh" *ort* rimes: *court, port, fort.* These I first employed quite self-consciously in my first consciously created Spenserian stanza-sonnet "Atlantis," on which I spent three years in all before I got it right, that is, all right in my own perception as the poet creating or "translating" it. Let me spread it all out here in terms of the rime words or, more accurately, the rime elements.

For the sake of style in subject matter and suitable tone, I insisted on the use of a few nautical or mildly "olden" words or terms: for ensample, *athwart* (pronounced *athort* or *athwort*) meaning across (as laid out across or upon), *empery* (as in empire or dominion), and *manifold* (as in multifarious, vaguely suggesting something beyond measure or strict accounting), not to forget the now forbidden phrase "of yore"! The rime scheme thus unfolds:—

Spenserian stanza: A B A B B C B C C:

rime elements: Ocean Sea / old / empery / in gold / enfold / court / manifold / port / fort

tercet: D C D: kings / court / things

couplet: E E: once of yore / western shore
(plus the codicil, which needs no diagramming)

This poem, incidentally, furnishes a good ensample of something that I learned from Leconte de Lisle: the use of a lyric to define or convey something epic in subject and/or emotion. I also learned the same thing from his disciple José-Maria de Heredia, who purveys it beautifully throughout the 118 sonnets making up *Les Trophées.*

Because such a variety of sound and language and meaning interpose between the first use of *court* and then the fourth and last use of it, the repetition becomes less obvious, particularly when read or recited aloud. If this is the audience's first exposure to the poem (rather than through the printed page), the reminiscence in rime actually helps the listener to grasp more clearly what the poem is expressing, a sense of infinite grief over something of great beauty or splendor irretrievably lost, and almost beyond the recall of mere words.

Somewhat later, when "translating" another poem but this time by a poet whom we first encounter as a prince, I created (at least in English) "When We Were Prince and Princess" as "Translated from the Atlantean of King Atlantarion I." In later ensamples of the Spenserian stanza-sonnet I have expanded the couplet to a quatrain and re-use the same rime words in successive stanzas, as follows:—

A B A   B C B
love / isles / love   smiles / rise / smiles

C D C   D E D
enterprise / throe / enterprise
                               long ago / ecstasy / long ago

F E F E   none / memory / one / eternity

 Here what might have been the couplet changed into a quatrain. Consciously, that is, to myself, I was varying the Spenserian stanza-sonnet form, but inadvertently I had created a new sonnet form in terza rima! Nonetheless, my loyalties remain with the Spenserian stanza-sonnet.

 Apart from the stanza (whatever shape it may take) as the basic agglutinative or combining structure, the poetic line in my own use and preference remains *the* basic structural element, and moreover, the end-stopped line, the rime thus imparting its appropriate or expected emphasis. I but rarely make use of runover lines, or enjambment, except to emphasize, or to feature, some symmetry, or a parallel rhetoric implicating a few or more lines.

 Since we are discussing it already, this is a good place to launch into the subject of rime and riming, as well as its role, along with that of meter, in making the resultant poetry much more incisive than what would otherwise obtain. Among the various kinds of rime there exist those of regular (or strict) rime, as well as of consonance and assonance, often and usually mixed up in actual poetic practice. Certain traditional poets today (sometimes excellent), for all their usage of rime and meter, might just as well write in free verse and free form, inasmuch as their usage does not always allow the reader or listener to "feel" the effect of that same rime and meter!

 The traditional poetic line, usually or often iambic pentameter (sometimes iambic hexameter), merits repeated mention. As observed by Timothy Steele (the doyen of the Neo-Formalists) in his manual on versification, iambic pentameter (especially since the reign of Elizabeth I) has become, and still is, the most versatile of all possible meters, capable of infinite variation, whether deployed by Spenser, Sidney, or Shakespeare (among legions of practitioners), but above all in dramatic blank verse.

We find in Shakespeare's own "sugared sonnets" an ideal exemplification of iambic pentameter, not just in terms of an ideal clarity, but especially in terms of an exceptional poetic music. Here are end-stopped lines galore whose rime words emphasize the meaning or sense of those lines, of what the poet states unequivocally, and with seeming ease. How deceptive that seeming ease of statement!

Beginning early in the Elizabethan period, in what usually passes for Early Modern English (even if one could argue that it really begins with Chaucer in one sense), we find the occasional poem (or mere piece of verse) that employs the fourteener (the fourteen-syllabic line), or more aptly, the alexandrine, which in English functions rather differently from what it does in French, because of the unavoidable difference in accentuation between the two languages. Sir Philip Sidney's posthumously published sequence of sonnets and other lyrics, *Astrophel and Stella,* as beautiful in its manner as anything similar by Shakespeare, opens with an exceptional (Petrarchan) sonnet cast in impeccable alexandrines. We skirt in respectful silence the *Polyolbion* of Michael Drayton: the monotony of how he handles his alexandrines remains unsurpassed, and a superb model not to imitate, amen.

Not until the latter 1800s and early 1900s, and among the English Symbolists, do we discover an especially artistic and variegated handling of the alexandrine. Lionel Johnson in particular has left us quite a few notable examples of often faultlessly conceived alexandrines. Nor should we forget Northern California's own Clark Ashton Smith. He has composed a notable number of poems employing the alexandrine with unusual expertise and appropriateness as found in *Ebony and Crystal, Sandalwood,* as well as later collections. We may cite as a supreme example his aptly titled lyric "Alexandrines." Smith profoundly savored the works of all manner of poets (in English), unfashionable, neglected, or simply forgotten, and he learned from all manner of unlikely writers.

In my own use of this poetic line, after eight years of studying French language and literature, the alexandrine came quite naturally to hand, if not instinctively. Nonetheless, I had to learn how to put it to use in English with its ever varying (and maddening) accentuation. In its quite spontaneous employment, while first utilizing the Spenserian stanza-sonnet, following the first nine lines (as embodied in the Spenserian stanza), I multiplied the number of syllables per line in lines 10-14 (the tercet and the couplet) as dictated by the emotion engendered by the subject matter. This discussion of the given poetic line and its place in the given poetic stanza yields inevitably here to a similar discussion of poetic form (and structure) in general, and of the given poetic forms (as I have used them) in particular.

Literary critics will occasionally speak of a piece of writing—essay, memoir, a book, a novel, an extended report, an expansive description, or whatever—as being in good form, or having this good form. By this term we might understand that they have found the writing in question attractive, well proportioned, and well arranged for maximum effect, whatever effect or goal the writer might have had in mind while composing the given piece or large-scale opus.

For some critics the same would remain true should they speak of some kind of traditional poetry, whatever the genre, whether of major or minor size and scope. Given whatever the genre or the form, the same critics might still speak of the poetic opus as being in good form. At least the concept of good form is not as elusive as that of good taste, but while one may teach something of good form, one can only suggest good taste. Even without an extraordinary teacher, the earnest student or disciple may learn on his own from a great piece of literary art.

For me it fell as a stroke of great good fortune that when I came to life as a beginning adult poet (having perused and studied much poetry in various languages) I was experiencing *The Faerie Queene* (during February or March through June of 1961) and at the same time simply rediscovering my native English as both a creative medium and as the common language of every day, particularly after concentrating on other languages and their bodies of accumulated literature, especially of poetry.

At the same time, beyond the usual quatrains (rhyming ABAB) or Petrarchan sonnets (rhyming ABBA ABBA CDE CDE) or whatever, I was taking a good hard look at Spenser's own forms as presented in *The Faerie Queene, The Shepheardes Calender,* and his other poetry. I directly found my own forms in those of *The Faerie Queene* above all: the Spenserian stanza, the Spenserian sonnet, as well as the alexandrine (ending each Spenserian stanza and sometimes a Spenserian sonnet) and the fourteener, or rather the old ballad metre (as embodied in the riming arguments preceding each canto).

I have thus consistently utilized these forms (from March 1961 until now, April 2017) throughout my five collections of poetry—stanza, sonnet, alexandrine, and fourteener—extrapolating in general from Spenser's own poetic practice and the models that his own works provide, but in terms of a modern audience as understood to be extant from the late 1800s on into the first quarter of the 2000s, and in terms of a continuous literary commonality during the same period.

Let us devote a few pages to the French Parnassians who flourished in the latter 1800s and early 1900s, that is, vis-à-vis Spenser and the English Renaissance. Even if in some respects they remain remarkably disparate groups, they both aspired to some kind of overall and overarching vision that could include literally everything. That might seem like a rather large order of poetic achievement for us to define, but not so much when reduced to essentials.

Spenser, Marlowe, Sidney, and Shakespeare, along with many other eminent intellectuals of their time, aspired (let us capitalize the phrase) toward a Syncretistic Concord or Harmony that included, or could include, everything: the cosmos, the planet, old worlds, novel worlds, the different forms of life, and so forth, even if they would not have defined things in general in quite that way. What we say about the Elizabethans can apply just as well to the French Parnassians, even if the latter would not have expressed it in the same way either.

The French Parnassians definitely stand out, given their overall time-frame, say, 1860 to 1900, and like the Elizabethans they, too, aspired toward some kind of universal vision, as alimented and supported by the scientific discoveries of their period. Whether English Renaissance or French Parnassus, all these poets originated in the Western World and partook of the general Christian outlook of their different historic periods, but the ever-skeptical French not so much, and but nominally.

As an important aside here, and as pointed out by C. S. Lewis, we should add that the Elizabethans, albeit Christians, but also syncretists, never dreamed of expounding what we might call their personal philosophies. Had you asked them, according to their own way of thinking, what they through they were achieving, they would probably have responded that what they were revealing was of course common wisdom, common knowledge, common experience. To do so, to reaffirm this commonality, was a duty, a public trust, a public service. To them this was more important than declaring a personal philosophy. Baudelaire and Leconte de Lisle certainly expounded their own personal philosophies, in our modern understanding of such; but the Parnassians as a group, also syncretistic in their own way, notably aspired toward an overall and overarching vision, whether optimistic or pessimistic (that is, in each case, in their poetry).

The French Parnassians not only aspired to this total vision, but also aspired intellectually to stand outside the regular humanistic framework of their century. This does not apply so much to José-Maria de Heredia as it does to his poetic master or teacher, Leconte de Lisle. Contrary to the general tradition of hope and optimistic expectation fomented by Christianity, Leconte de Lisle espoused an especially virulent form of cosmic pessimism, but not shared by Heredia as the master's leading disciple, possibly due to the more fortunate circumstances of the Cuban-born poet's life and career.

This is a cosmic pessimism that absolutely does not flatter the human species, nor cater to it in any manner. It is fascinating to notice and ponder that Ashton Smith arrived at a similar stance (as a result of an enormous amount of reading and evidently profound contemplation) but with a far greater degree of compassion and sympathy than what Leconte de Lisle could ever have mustered. Whether consciously or not, even before he might have investigated the religion, Ashton Smith had already veered instinctively toward a Buddhist perspective. Buddhism (an extension of Hinduism) is the only major system of belief (unlike Christianity or Islam) that does not, and has not, committed violence toward other human beings or, for that matter, toward any other form of life.

Such a stance has a huge potential to combat the worst forms of anthropocentrism and its inherent arrogance. The cosmic pessimism of Leconte de Lisle, Ashton Smith, and H. P. Lovecraft has much to recommend it—how different, refreshing, and existential!—and if I aspire toward it myself, I do so honestly and sincerely. The cosmos does not revolve around the human species and its small-scale concerns of religion, art, philosophy, literature, and so forth. I personally take great comfort in the fact that to date the human species can wreak no great damage to the cosmos, apart from our planet, and that the cosmos at best is quite indifferent to us.

If the cosmos all at once snuffed us all out, the entire human race, just like a candle flame, we would not know the difference after the fact, and no one or nothing else would miss us. I love human beings individually, but I do not love the human species. Lest I be misunderstood, let me cite a parallel example. Once when profoundly irritated by her mother, but not expressing it except to me—her mother had temporarily gone out of the room—a woman friend said, "I love my mother, but I do not always like her." Precisely!

To return to myself and my small-scale concerns as a poet traditional or traditionalist. (The vast size of the cosmos puts everything in perspective!) The reason why I like using a form like a sonnet is no mystery. It is like a small but acutely focused vignette that opens a door or a gate onto what I propose to bring to attention and in suitable detail. Having created my own sonnet form and my own kind of blank verse, having revived several forms otherwise neglected, I certainly intended to use them, and I have done so. I shall continue to do so as long as I can. Even if I complete no further collections, I shall still turn out some piece or other of poetry.

H. P. Lovecraft—A Belated Homage

Even if I have at least mentioned Lovecraft in some of my essays—going recently through a collection of them, as well as of miscellaneous reviews—I realized with a shock that I had never written a separate piece on him, a piece in tribute to him and his voluminous writings, not only his fiction and poetry, his essays, and his monumental study "Supernatural Horror in Literature," but also the enormous quantity of letters that he addressed to a wide variety of friends and acquaintances, many of them fellow scriveners with a strong interest like Lovecraft in fantastic stories, often of horror, often supernatural.

The emergence of the pulp magazines in the 1920s and 1930s, particularly *Weird Tales* (1923-54), provided willy-nilly the market for stories that could not find easy publication elsewhere. Then the similar rise of the science-fiction pulps in the 1930s, especially *Wonder Stories,* provided another market where imagination could take wing and flourish. That these magazines published many mediocre stories as well, or less than mediocre, means nothing in one sense—that is beside the point—but they also published a great many stories of often high literary calibre.

Some of the contributors of the better stories to these magazines have now grown in literary acceptance, even outside the literary ghetto that first gave them prominence. We need mention only a handful or so of these writers, names now rather well known and celebrated in the U.S. and internationally, such as H. P. Lovecraft, C. Ashton Smith, Robert E. Howard, Henry S. Whitehead, August Derleth, R. H. Barlow, Manly Wade Wellman, Ray Bradbury, and so forth. Due to the devotion of one of these writers, August Derleth, to the writings of another, H. P. Lovecraft—above all to the remarkable fantastic stories penned by the latter—Arkham House came into existence in the late 1930s and early 1940s to give regular book publication and hence greater permanence to the fiction of Lovecraft and writers of similar merit.

It was not happenstance that created Arkham House in Sauk City, some twenty miles or so northwest of the state capital, Madison, in southern Wisconsin. Sauk City was the home of the fledgling regionalist August Derleth, soon to become one of Wisconsin's foremost writers, such as he remains to this day. Meanwhile, supported from the sales of the Arkham House books, and also by Derleth himself as the owner-editor, out of the earnings from his multifarious writings during the 1950s, the small publishing house remained extant somehow. Then during the 1960s the financial situation reversed itself, and perhaps as a species of cosmic justice, Arkham House helped support the owner-editor himself.

If the aficionados of the pulp magazines of the 1930s and 1940s represent the so-called First Fandom, then I in the mid-1950s must represent (as a token figure) Second Fandom. It just so happened that at the midpoint in the middle decade (of the 1950s) I discovered Lovecraft and his tales via various fantasy and science-fiction anthologies edited by Derleth. Then I found, beyond and via the same, Arkham House and its unique publications. This discovery changed my life and eventually made me into the poet and scholar that I remain to this day.

Thus my first debt for this fruitful direction is to Lovecraft, Derleth, and Arkham House, but above all to Lovecraft for his wonderful stories of fantasy and supernatural horror, and then for his no less extraordinary guidebook "Supernatural Horror in Literature," a paramount manual for me both in subject matter and style. Quite apart from my own personal evolution as an author, I have observed with a certain pride, as a fellow New Englander, how Lovecraft's name and fame have increased throughout the enormous Anglophone world, and concomitantly outside of it as well through translation. This greater fame, and how it has grown, makes an impressive saga quite by itself, and involved many factors and many persons.

By now (April 2017) I have read and re-read much of Lovecraft's literary output many times over, but never again with quite the original thrill with which I first encountered the first stories from his pen, here not a figure of speech, but literal. He actually wrote most of his fiction with pen and ink, and then translated it (that is, changed it) into regular typescript. While he wrote fluently by hand with pen, the typing per se (evidently of the hunt-and-peck method) seems always to have proven an ordeal for him.

Thus, if we say that he hammered out his stories with great pains, we speak the plain truth. I for one rejoice that Lovecraft went to all the annoying trouble to pen and then to type out his stories, although he happily consigned the task of typing (from his handwritten and quite legible manuscripts) to others (for example, Donald Wandrei) when they offered to do so. But let me return to the initial thrill—and I do mean thrill!—that H.P.L.'s prose fictions engendered in myself when I first read and experienced them. Let me review some of those titles.

"The Colour out of Space": I first read this in some science-fiction anthology edited by Derleth. I read, then re-read, and yet read it again, astounded by its science-fiction or science-fantasy perspective as expressed in an elaborate and yet original style reminiscent of Edgar Allan Poe. "The Rats in the Walls": more obviously Poesque, this reveals the same obsessive power palpably felt in "The Colour out of Space," but whereas the first story liberated me out into the cosmos, the second story drove me back into myself in a claustrophobic manner. I wanted more stories like the first! "The Haunter of the Dark" provided me with a double thrust, both inward and outward. Something invoked from outer space invades the seeker's own earthbound existence, and to his destruction.

Soon after these and other stories that represented my first serious encounter with Lovecraft's cosmic muse—a muse freed from the shackles of the older religions and philosophies—I first discovered and read the great science-fiction and supernatural novellas and novels that H.P.L. had written. "The Shadow out of Time": this narrative contains one of the most shattering climaxes (emotional and spiritual) in all fiction, when the protagonist realizes that what he has understood as no more than a dream reveals itself as a memory of something he had actually lived in a previous incarnation happening in a remote corner of the illimitable universe. *The Case of Charles Dexter Ward:* when this narrative was not frightening me to death with its necromantic overtones and surprises, it was charming me with its lyrical evocations of New England and its landscape, such as I had never quite encountered in the area's elder poets, e.g., J. R. Lowell, Longfellow, R. W. Emerson, and so forth. "The Shadow over Innsmouth": this extended tale hit me particularly hard with its oceanic overtones (and undertones) concerning ocean life and fisheries, originating as I did in old New Bedford in southeast Massachusetts with its commercial fishing long established and of great scope. Last but not least, *At the*

Mountains of Madness: this account occurs mostly in the remote reaches of Antarctica, as alien an environment with its coldness and its dominant species of penguins as any world far beyond our own planet.

Later, thanks to Rah Hoffman's personal book collection, I could read, and concentrate upon, what had become my very own favorites from among H.P.L.'s distinctive fictional output, his so-called Dunsanian stories, generally much shorter than the novels already mentioned, except for *The Dream-Quest of Unknown Kadath:* although markedly Dunsanian, it generates its own separate appeal. Again later, when thanks to the same collection I read most of Dunsany's own output, I realized that Lovecraft's own Dunsanian tales, often rich in poetry of narrative and atmosphere, remain in many ways noticeably different from Dunsany's own stories. Among my own favorites in this part of Lovecraft's *oeuvre* I rank rather highly "The Cats of Ulthar," "The Quest of Iranon," "Polaris," along with others.

Somewhere along this itinerary of literary exploration and discovery I first met his poetry. While competent and professional, as well as often agreeably Poesque in style and metre, it did not hit me as hard as his prose fictions. That is, until I discovered the pure gold of *Fungi from Yuggoth,* one of the most exceptional sonnet sequences ever written, each piece a separate story (or a part of one), and each sonnet a gem. As Fritz Leiber and I both agreed—in the course of our many discussions about Lovecraft, Ashton Smith, R. E. Howard, H. S. Whitehead, Ray Bradbury, and so forth—*Fungi from Yuggoth* is great modern poetry despite its evocation of an antiquity nearly beyond imagination. The opening and closing sonnets have retained a far greater poignancy than what H.P.L. himself might have consciously engineered or anticipated.

In spite of the negative comments and critiques of his *oeuvre* by well-intentioned or ill-purposed Zoiluses, Lovecraft's writings have definitely endured and will probably endure well into the future. They have already outlasted the animadversions of a great critic like Edmund Wilson, and have also earned the admiring respect of distinguished critics in France like Jean Cocteau. We must value the praise coming from such a Protean creative figure as Cocteau, particularly vis-à-vis Edmund Wilson. Incidentally, I am a grateful admirer of the last-cited man of letters, some of whose reviews have served me as a major source of insight and information, especially a long and exceptional essay on Swinburne as poet, playwright, and Francophone. But when we consider all the buzz and fuss about H. P. L. and J. R. R. Tolkien at conventions continuing for quite a few years now—the critic in question simply did not understand the works of either of these cult figures—let us ponder the fact that no one has yet organized a single convention in honor of Edmund Wilson, never mind an ongoing annual one. Lovecraft's best and most idiosyncratic work will outlast that of many writers acclaimed and lauded lavishly in their own time.

For my part, I cherish much of H.P.L.'s unusual and beautiful writing as found in his poems in prose, and in such of his prose fictions that find rank as extended poems in prose—the Dunsanian tale "The Quest of Iranon" (remarkably similar to Ashton Smith's own story "Xeethra") forms a perfect example. Lovecraft's remarkable powers of imagination, language, and expression cause not only his shorter tales to stand out, but also the novels already enumerated, as well as many others not mentioned. Even if he died in relative obscurity, Lovecraft did not quite pass into oblivion, thanks to such partisans as August Derleth and Donald Wandrei and the publishing firm they established together, Arkham House.

Flickering Shadows on a Lighted Screen

In my recent autobiography *Hobgoblin Apollo* (more Hobgoblin than Apollo!) I record the considerable presence and influence that movies played in my life from early childhood (at the age of three) into early adolescence (at the age of thirteen, when I entered high school). However, the movies actually exerted a far greater influence than what I have already recounted or realized earlier. I speak of both my perception of life and my aesthetic sense. The often excellent art direction displayed in many feature films of the 1930s (particularly for me, when the studios would re-release them in the 1940s) and then the new productions of the 1940s themselves definitely nourished my sense of aesthetics. How could they not have? Both my parents worked in movie houses: my father managed a first-run theatre, and my mother worked as box-office cashier in a second-run house. I witnessed many films in both venues, not to mention special excursions to other theatres exhibiting extraordinary films not shown where my parents worked. This essay then deals with my moviegoing in greater detail.

Many film critics and film historians agree today that the Hollywood feature films made in the 1930s and 1940s (not all of them spectaculars) make up some kind of Golden Age. I did not see my first movie (in the company of my brother Ronald) until age three (he, age four). This was the then unprecedented full-scale animated cartoon *Snow White and the Seven Dwarfs* in 1937. I do recall witnessing many outstanding movies beginning in the early 1940s. Even if I could not have seen those made and released in the 1930s, I did catch them on the rebound (as it were) when re-released. That way I could experience them, even if as a kid, when everything is a given, I did not consciously register them as having had someone write, direct, art-design, and "musick" them, beyond the actors animating them.

Even if on occasion we could get to see a rare foreign film (usually British), most of the new films of the 1940s, as well as those of the 1930s in re-release, emanated from the major Hollywood studios—MGM, Paramount, Warner Brothers, Twentieth-Century Fox—and the occasional smaller but strategically important studio such as the one named David O. Selznick. We did notice the name of at least one major British studio, J. Arthur Rank. That studio released some of the more spectacular British films of the late 1930s and early 1940s, that is, such as I can recall from that time in my life as an uncritical child.

In general we may state unequivocally that many films of this period could not have succeeded popularly and artistically to the extent that they did without their often outstanding art direction (directly affecting the regular direction and the visual style of the photography). The music often played an important determining role in the film's emotional impact. Even if not always officially credited, William Cameron Menzies (1896–1957) through his overall art design immediately affected the "look" and hence the "feel" of many of the exceptional feature films of the 1930s and 1940s, both British and American.

If in my recollections I indicate precise dates and names, I do so simply as a guide for myself. My brother and I had not yet started school when we witnessed *Snow White and the Seven Dwarfs* in 1937, a huge gamble on Walt Disney's part, which nonetheless paid off very well indeed. He could now proceed to make similar full-scale animated cartoons; the next one remains one of my own favorites, even more so than *Snow White,* to wit, *Pinocchio* (1940). The imagination and invention it displayed in the clockwork of all types in the woodcarver Geppetto's atelier enchanted and haunted me.

In that same year of 1940 an even more extraordinary film made its début, *Fantasia,* an original but viable mixture of classical music and animation, which did not do so well at the box office when first released, but which gradually became a cult favorite and ultimately paid back the original investment. It more than succeeded artistically, especially as enhanced by Deems Taylor, the composer, as narrator. *Snow White, Pinocchio,* and *Fantasia* certainly impressed my brother and me, unsophisticated though we might have been.

The other early feature film that I recall us witnessing is *The Wizard of Oz* (1939), when I was five, my brother six. That was the same year in which *Gone with the Wind* made its long-awaited début, even if I could not have seen it then. Only adults could grasp and appreciate an adult feature film (and at such a length) as this one. How far distant in mood and feeling from *The Wizard of Oz,* not to overlook Disney's other later classic *Bambi* (1942), which I only witnessed years into the future during my early adolescence. Also years later, when I first witnessed *Gone with the Wind* (in the later 1940s), I learned that the film's overall appearance owed quite a bit to William Cameron Menzies (if memory serves).

Menzies it certainly was who masterminded the art direction of many exceptional British films of the later 1930s and early 1940s. Besides art direction he also directed several films, including the early science-fiction classic *Things to Come* (1936), which had the added benefit of music by Arthur Bliss. Based on H. G. Wells's narrative *The Shape of Things to Come,* the distinctive look that Menzies achieved for this film exercised a strong influence on many later sci-fi movies good, great, and bad. His art design (and sometimes partial direction) played a major part in some lavish adventure films that intrigued me, but which I did not always understand in terms of plot and adult motivation. All that I can recall about the J. Arthur Rank feature films that identified them to me as such was the half-naked man who hits a gong at the start of each film as a kind of logo.

No matter that I did not always understand the plot of some of these movies. They seemed spectacular to me, and all the more so because of their Technicolor photography. At the time they seemed to come forth in cornucopia-like profusion, as directed or somehow masterminded by one or more of the three Korda brothers (apparently geniuses), Zoltan, Alexander, and Vincent: *The Four Feathers* (1939), *The Thief of Bagdad* (1940), and *The Jungle Book* (1942). The superb performances by C. Aubrey Smith and Ralph Richardson distinguish the grand adventure narrative of *The Four Feathers.* In *The Thief of Bagdad* the performance of Rex Ingram as the Genie, no less than that of Conrad Veidt as the arch-evil Grand Vizier of Bagdad, turned out as notable as that of the lithe and nimble Sabu as the thief himself. The magical milieu and character of the boy Mowgli (raised by wolves in the jungles of India), as played by the ever charismatic Sabu, made this *Jungle Book* a classic for that period, thanks to the necromancy of the Korda brothers. The music by their compatriot Hungarian, the distinguished composer Miklos Rozsa, enormously increased the visceral and aesthetic impact of these three films. Somewhat later, hired by MGM, Rozsa arrived in Hollywood, where he became the great composer at that studio.

Even if invariably disdained by critics like Gilbert Highet, the lavish and spectacular films of Cecil B. DeMille, released through Paramount Studios and featured regularly at the Olympia Theatre, which my father managed, loomed no less large in my life than those masterminded by the Korda brothers. Re-released in the 1940s, I witnessed *The Sign of the Cross* (1933) and *The Crusades* (1935). The *Cleopatra* of 1934 I did not witness until my senior year in high school, during the winter of 1952–53.

Also in re-release during the 1940s, I discovered DeMille's *echt-* Americana films *The Plainsman* (1937) and *Union Pacific* (1939), culminating in *Northwest Mountain Police* (1940) and *Reap the Wild Wind* (1942), his response to *Gone with the Wind* (1939). Although resourcefully made and with real flair as ever, *Reap the Wild Wind* could not compare in plot with the sweep and impact of the earlier film. Starting with *Northwest Mounted Police,* DeMille had all his later feature films photographed in Technicolor: *The Story of Dr. Wassell* (1944), *Unconquered* (1947), *Samson and Delilah* (1950), *The Greatest Show on Earth* (1952), and *The Ten Commandments* (1956). Quite a few of DeMille's later films had music by Victor Young, starting with *Reap the Wild Wind.* Although not up to the higher standard, say, of Max Steiner, Miklos Rozsa, and Bernard Herrmann, Young's average score functioned well enough in any DeMille movie (this was during the 1940s).

By the latter 1940s and early 1950s, going to the movies (usually for free) at two different movie houses had lost much of its appeal for me, as I became ever more involved with my studies in high school, and then with other subjects while in the military (Lovecraft, Arkham House, etc.), but continuing with my languages. On occasion I would still take in a superior feature film. One in particular stands out from the 1950s, to wit, *Beneath the 12-Mile Reef* (1953), especially remarkable for the underwater photography in Cinemascope and the magically evocative music by Bernard Herrmann, the great composer at Twentieth-Century Fox in the same fashion as Miklos Rozsa at MGM.

That was one of the few movies at that period that I paid good money to witness again and again, following it from a movie palace in downtown Jacksonville (then in the military, I was stationed a little west of the big city) all the way to a remote movie house in one of the suburbs north of the downtown. The main plot of the film, involving

Terry Moore and Robert Wagner as lovers, I could barely tolerate, although the subplot involving Gilbert Roland as the father and Robert Wagner as the son proved very moving indeed, especially when the father dies as the result of an undersea accident. The story concerns rival families or factions of sponge fishers off the Florida coast as focused in and around the 12-mile reef in the title.

What attracted me to this movie? The unusually evocative music by Bernard Herrmann. (You can purchase a separate CD of the music today.) I remember reading in *Time* or some such magazine of the 1950s that Herrmann in the sections of the music mirroring the underwater sequences had employed no fewer than nine harps. (The composer himself had conducted the studio orchestra for the film.) The ravishing sound thus created remains what attracted me to the film in the first place!

But I have almost forgotten to mention what happened to become salient among my very favorite movies of all from the middle 1930s to the middle 1950s: disaster or catastrophe films! The Hollywood studios of the time made them in such a way that they somehow seem far more authentic than most later catastrophe movies. Apart from the first three (which I witnessed only in re-release), I watched the remaining four when first released. In general these movies build up to the given disaster as a dramatic climax. *San Francisco* (1936) features a truly grandiose earthquake, followed by an all-consuming fire. *The Hurricane* (1937) demonstrates a typhoon to end all typhoons. *In Old Chicago* (1937) presents the great Chicago conflagration as a fire to end all fires. *The Rains Came* (1939) depicts a quadruple catastrophe: the heavy monsoon rains, an earthquake, the local big dam breaking, and the resultant big flood. (The tiny Maria Ouspenskaya as the Maharani awed me almost more than the catastrophes.) *Titanic* (1953) features the inevitable iceberg collision followed by the big liner taking its nose dive beneath the ocean. *The Naked Jungle* (1954) parades a broad procession of red army ants that evidently measures several miles in length. *Elephant Walk* (1954): someone has built the big house of a tea plantation in Ceylon across a former elephant route that the herd reclaims, rampaging through the mansion and setting it on fire by knocking down several lighted lanterns, or what have you. Now that is a proper catastrophe for you disaster-hounds!

Intangibility

Intangibility? Untouchability, and in the arts? What might that mean? Or rather, what can it mean, as applied to the arts, fine or performing or elsewise? It has an immediate application in a commercial gallery, where the gallery owners and the artists whose work is on display proffer likely specimens, pictorial and sculptural, for purchase. On rare occasions some sculptures may have a sign on them, inviting the onlooker to touch them, to feel them, thus an unaccustomed chance to put physical sensuality to the test. Such sculptures as I have experienced in this invitational manner are often abstract and polished so as to render the physical touch itself smooth and easily accessible to digital exploration and appreciation.

Intangible or untouchable in a museum setting literally means "Do not touch," or do not get too close, as many signs will remind the spectator. Such prohibition serves an obvious and much needed purpose. Many museumgoers will visit a museum for a particular (traveling) exhibit, or they will enter some historical museum next to an historical site so that they can see close up the artistic or other materials recovered from the given site. For purposes of protection and preservation, the museum authorities must often put the historical specimens under glass in display cases. The guards on duty will sometimes admonish the spectator not to get too close if the materials are out in the open. All very well and good.

I recall a special episode as a museumgoer visiting an historical museum right next to, or not far from, the given historical site. I was passing a week or so in Lyon, the gourmand capital of France, staying at a midrange hotel in the chief part of the old city, at the conjunction of the two rivers, where the Saône flows into the Rhône. To the west, fairly high up, across the Saône, lay the extensive flat area, a kind of mini-plateau, where the considerable ruins yet stood erect of the ancient Roman forum of Lyon, then called Lugdunum. I hasten to assure the reader that I was not on the scene for the gourmandise (although the food seemed excellent) so much as I had come there to conduct some genealogical research on behalf of my maternal grandfather's family, the Teillières, primarily farmers. They had lived in Lyonnais, but I discovered nothing about them.

Nonetheless, I enjoyed the ancient Roman ambiance and the nearby museum. A bespectacled college student, as a mixture of guard and curator, sat on duty at some desk or table. When I entered the chief exhibit space, we nodded at each other in acknowledgment. I began looking intensely at the sculptures and other objects recovered from the forum, some of it arresting or curious indeed. I was examining a bas-relief attached to a wall, and at easily accessible eye-level. I became so fascinated that I had unconsciously moved myself very close to the sculpture (incidentally, very well done).

It must have seemed to the student guard-curator that I stood so close that I was virtually touching the bas-relief with my face. Well, not quite. The student came over to me where I stood wrapt in my aesthetic and archaeological reverie. He startled me when he spoke, admonishing me not to stand so close, lest with my breath or flesh I might perpetrate some damage on the sculpture inadvertently. I pulled back, with astonishment writ large on my countenance. I thanked him for his admonition. Thus we have here one instance of museumistic warning, "Do not touch."

But at the opposite extreme we now present, in a different vein, another instance of untouchability or intangibility. We speak of music, whether live or in some recorded form. This difference results from the very nature, the physical quality, of the art involved, an art whose product we cannot literally touch, but that we can register through one of the five senses, in this case the sense of hearing. However, as we know, music at an evolved level does not come cheap, especially classical music in the concert hall, the opera house, or in any other type of suitable theatre. Such music demands highly trained personnel, often educated over a long period of time, whether instrumentalists or as opera singers of any kind for any type of developed musical theatre.

What could outclass or equal music as an intangible something but whose value any sensitive person can feel, except perhaps the trained voices and mannerisms of trained actors? Wealthy people have often established considerable endowments for the arts, the performing arts above all. Other people bequeath a major part of their estates for the same purpose. They do this not only to maintain the group of performers at a certain strength—the instrumentalists, the singers, the dancers, and the actors—but just as much to establish schools or academies where future performers can receive the needed and prolonged training. Whether involving music or not, none of this comes cheap, as declared earlier. The whole apparatus of classical culture also requires trained personnel as administrators to handle the money with care and with due regard for both the long term and the short. Ticket sales may help, but they can, and do, not cover all the expenses. Even totalitarian governments have recognized this fact, and as in the case of Russia have lavishly supported the performing arts, inherited from the Tsarist period.

All this may seem obvious and commonplace, but in a variety of ways it is not and needs reiteration. When a concertgoer attends some subscription concert in some symphony hall to hear and experience a diverse program of symphonic music from whatever source, a great amount of time, energy, and money has been expended so that the concertgoer can enjoy that certain experience of something that cannot be touched or apprehended except through one or more of the individual's own apparatus of the five senses. Impalpable to actual physical touch. So, what price intangibility?

That's Hollywood? That's Hollywood!

Some ten or twelve miles as the bird flies northwest of the grand municipal center of Los Angeles there lies the town (actually well-inhabited city) officially named and known as Hollywood—thus christened, it would seem, by some real-estate genius back in the 1920s who called the area then being developed Hollywoodland. Either he or someone else had a big sign erected that spelled out the name Hollywoodland in giant letters painted white, a sign easily perceived across the Hollywood hills (actually low mountains), or more specifically located on Mount Lee, but also better known sometimes as Mount Hollywood. The giant letters now stand recently refurbished and repainted.

Hollywood is thus a real place, a real town, but it is also a tremendous concept (denoting art and entertainment) that embraces a much wider area, indeed much of Los Angeles at large, given the once major movie studios that dominated the overall region, the big studios with their giant sound stages (many still intact and busy still with movies or television programs in process of production or manufacture). These are the old studios with names like MGM (Culver City), Twentieth-Century Fox (their once enormous lot now transformed into Century City), Paramount (actually close to, or in, the town of Hollywood), and Warner Brothers (in the San Fernando Valley north of central L.A.).

During the decades of the 1920s or 1930s, lasting on through the 1960s and 1970s, these studios, as well as many smaller ones, created an enormous number of feature and co-feature films, documentaries, and so forth, many remarkably good, many remarkably bad—with many of them continuing to have an endless life (it would appear) on television, with an exceptional few occasionally re-released for movie houses. In fact, many television companies such as CBS, NBC, RCA, etc., continue to utilize the old sound stages of the big studios, as well as the new facilities; thus many of the new television studios are transmogrified from the leading radio facilities.

Even if on occasion I would have contact with people working at the old movie studios or the new television ones, I rarely encountered anyone or anything directly connected with both the old and the new locales of seemingly monolithic Hollywood—with one salient exception, a person whom I met in May of 1961 (via Forrie Ackerman) through our mutual interest in California poet and fictioneer Clark Ashton Smith, soon to die in August of that same year. This intermediary between Smith and myself was Rah Hoffman.

As we got to know each other, we discussed how close C.A.S. came to being better known during the late 1930s or early 19040s. Universal Studios (according to report) seriously considered making two of Smith's novellas into super-thriller feature films, *The Dark Eidolon* and *The Colossus of Ylourgne*. Had Universal actually made either or both stories into feature films, it not only would have focused attention on Smith as poet and fictioneer, but it would have made him financially much better off than at any other time in his life or career.

Even if Universal was one of the many studios where Rah worked on occasion as a film cutter or editor, he never was able to verify this report about the two Smith novellas being made into regular feature films, although he did check it out as best he could under the circumstances, that is, as his job allowed him to do so. As Rah often reminded me, D.S.F. with his head often lost somewhere in the clouds, the movies as well as television exist as businesses first and foremost. Even if their chief objective consists in creating films or programs as entertainment, they remain big businesses run and managed as any large commercial operation usually is, dominated by hard-edged thinking preoccupied with making maximum profits. No mystery there.

My own main contact with Hollywood the town occurred when I would go there to frequent a wonderful big bookstore called Larry Edmunds, where among other items I picked up for ten dollars or so a near mint copy (with mint dust jacket) of Cyril Beaumont's massive monograph, the *Complete Book of Ballets* (the second edition). This book emporium specialized in books on movies, the theatre, and the entertainment arts. Otherwise, during the years that I lived in some part of the enormous L.A. basin, 1955-65, I had little contact, nor did I desire it particularly, with the Hollywood world. I knew Hollywood as an industry spread out all over the L.A. basin and sometimes beyond.

It was, and it remains, a business! But to be fair and evenhanded, I must also state that a Hollywood film has also managed to be every now and then genuine art, as achieved by the occasional director of genius, or by such an exceptional creative director and producer as David O. Selznick.

As for famous people or places associated with Hollywood, I had my share of encounters during 1955–65. Given the film industry everywhere (sometimes using U.C.L.A. as a typical academic setting for movies or television), it was near impossible not to run into Hollywood people and places. One weekend while walking down Westwood Boulevard just south of U.C.L.A.'s main entrance on the south, I ran across the actor Glenn Ford, the seeming antithesis of movie glamour with a heavy five o'clock shadow, and wearing some blue jeans and a short jacket made of the same material. We passed each other with a nod and a smile.

On another occasion my partner Bob Crook and I with another couple of guys visited a well-known star. This couple lived in Hancock Park, an older, somewhat fancy neighborhood between Beverly Hills and downtown L.A. with big beautiful homes located on big lush-green lots. We visited this other couple every now and then. On one occasion per their arrangement we met with them and in our separate cars drove up to visit some special and handsome friends of theirs at their unpretentious but pleasant home somewhere in the San Fernando Valley. This was Tab Hunter and his then partner, where the four of us (the two couples) had dinner with our hosts in their house. They had prepared the meal themselves. Yes, it was good, it was tasty (something with ground beef).

What made the dinner special? It was that one of our hosts was in fact Tab Hunter, who when we made our entrance (his partner let us in and greeted us warmly) had been sitting and reading some ponderous-looking book while he wore his reading spectacles. Tab appeared serious and sober (we did have wine with dinner) and very pleasant withal. We talked about everything under the sun. Like the four guests, our hosts were liberal in politics and lifestyle. If memory serves, we did not discuss movies, but the television documentary series *Victory at Sea*. We all agreed that Richard Rodgers's music (as arranged, or rather composed, by Robert Russell Bennett) made the individual episodes of the series outstanding and cohesive. While our friends from Hancock Park returned home, Bob and I went back to the domicile that we shared in Pacific Palisades north of Santa Monica.

Another notable event occurred when I met my warm and amiable friend Angelo Graham at the gym I patronized on Wilshire Boulevard in Santa Monica. Of Greek descent, his real birth name was Evangelos Grammatikos. He worked in the Art Department at Twentieth-Century Fox. We became fast friends, and at some point he invited me to have lunch with him at the commissary or cafeteria where he usually ate at Fox. After lunch he took me in his car on a tour of the old, enormous Fox studio lot divided into two major parts (bisected by a big boulevard, Wilshire or Santa Monica), where he pointed out many old sets once used in various movies, as for example the French village in *The Song of Bernadette* with Jennifer Jones. Last we visited the Art Department where he worked, and he showed me the miniature models (made out of balsa wood) of the sets for the big "double" movie *Cleopatra* (1963), depicting the adventures of Julius Caesar and Mark Antony with the Egyptian queen. Angelo himself had worked on some of the sets.

Then I went back home by bus to Pacific Palisades via Santa Monica as usual. Earlier before I met Angelo for lunch, I had gone to the personnel department, where I had applied for any kind of a job at the studio, but they were not hiring at that time. Had *Cleopatra* tanked, it would have ended Fox. (I myself preferred DeMille's version of 1934.) The owners of Fox realized a huge sum of money when they sold the huge studio lot (both halves) for a real-estate development that became Century City. That just about sums up my genuine Hollywood encounters, but my days in L.A. were numbered. I would move to Northern California (to Auburn before later moving to San Francisco) in response to the outré prose and poetry of one C. Ashton Smith. Even though Smith no longer lived in Auburn, I had already resided and worked there during a summer job, and I had already begun the research for the Smith bibliography there.

Farewell to All That

Well, not quite!

When a writer attains a certain age and finds it an almost impossibly difficult challenge to write anything and everything of a simple nature (never mind without complications) in some cogent and coherent form, then the time has come for that writer *not* to abandon writing but simply to cut back on the amount of writing to be done or attempted.

What I write here is a personal note, a personal essay, with which to close this little collection of essays concerning the subject of aesthetics as directly impinging on my own life. At eighty-two and a half years old, or somewhat more, I realize that I am no longer eighteen! I have just completed my two last books (at least in manuscript), and I realize that I might as well give up now the thought of any further books per se from my pen, typewriter, or word-processor.

This is a simple recognition of limits. At a certain point in my current life, when basic mentation and remembrance appear to pose a near insuperable challenge, then I realize all the more not to abandon *all* writing but to concentrate on smaller tasks, an essay, a brief memoir, a poem, a poem in prose, maybe a short story, or some other short piece of fiction—something that I can actually accomplish without spending an inordinate amount of time, effort, and energy to do so.

For myself as a not overly ambitious but idealistic poet and scrivener, to surrender the potential of any further books (the major hope or ambition of any writer worth his own salt and essential minerals) represents a difficult acknowledgment, a melancholy recognizance. However, words, thoughts, phrases, invention, and imagination have ceased coming to me with any ease. Poetry in fixed form is a different matter, because there the writer expects the need for writing and rewriting, not that it always turns into a task of travail.

When I needs must consult the dictionary for words and spellings that I have known all my life (well, at least since kindergarten), and then forget the results as soon as I leave the dictionary, such is the time to work exclusively on small morceaux, prose or poetry, such as

I can still accomplish. For me this is the reality that I now face and cannot escape; and I shall act accordantly, as much as I can, with taste and intelligence.

Meanwhile I can still write, I can still read, I can still edit, I can still study, I can relearn all the languages that I learned long ago during my youth and young adulthood. All that remains as a great consolation, as the greatest of consolations.

Also meanwhile, among big projects not quite finished, I must pursue the final stages of finding publication for my magnum opus, *The Case of the Light Fantastic Toe*. First, I must complete going over the entire printed text (as realized by Lulu Enterprises) yet one more time, before submitting it to the suitable publishers, whoever they turn out to be, following their inspection and then possible acceptance of that massive enterprise.

—D. SIDNEY-FRYER

Auburn, California,
16 April 2017.

Codicil

In the event that I might not have sufficiently explained myself in other essays and other writings, that is, those that have attained publication: I should state here in this epistemological context (if thus I might express myself) what I currently think I accomplished by pursuing a career and a life as a poet and a poet-performer, no less than as a scrivener of other materials.

It took me from 1961 on into 1971 to create and publish (i.e., have published for me) the First Series of *Songs and Sonnets Atlantean*. Despite an early and very negative reaction to family life and marriage (as observed by myself living among and as part of the working poor), I broke my vow never to marry and father any children. Luckily no children appeared, and around or after my divorce (from Gloria Kathleen Braly), I returned to the celibate condition, and (I must say) with a huge sense of relief. Personally I was not made for family life, to function as a paterfamilias. I had nothing as a provider to offer a woman, and I did not want any children. More than six or seven billion human beings exist on the planet Earth, and ergo why should I want to add to that sum total?

It probably happened at this critical juncture that I renewed my vow never again to get involved in a long-term relationship beyond pure friendship without sustained intimacy with man or woman. Then after that momentous decision (if not renunciation) I continued writing poetry that resulted in the Second Series, then the Third Series, and then at long last the Trilogy, *The Atlantis Fragments* (2008, 2009). More recently my autobiography made its appearance, *Hobgoblin Apollo,* the volume concluding with another poetry collection *Odds and Ends.*

In a similar fashion I proffer the present volume, opening with a modest gathering of essays on the arts, *Aesthetics Ho!,* and concluding with another poetry collection, *Ends and Odds.* As just previously discussed, this will probably remain my final book, qua book, because my current mentation cannot any longer achieve the major project that a regular book involves. Nonetheless I can as a writer continue to produce little pieces, essay, poem in verse, poem in prose, and so forth. I can also continue as a poet-performer, preaching the Gospel of Poetry, as expressed in Edwin Markham's memorable phrase, quaint-sounding but perfectly accurate.

Appendix

Appendix

Songs and Sonnets Atlantean, by Donald S. Fryer, Arkham House, 1971, 131 pp., $5.00.
Review by Mark Purcell. *Luna Monthly,* December 1972.

S&SA is a very amiable, kooky book: with its text of poems and purple prose, literary and legendary history, and on the back cover its author, an ex-Marine, posed in Buena Vista Park [in San Francisco] as an Elizabethan courtier. Some of the problems S&SA causes a reviewer can be explained by saying that it is presumably the first book on the Atlantis legend in Renaissance France that can be recommended primarily to readers or librarians buying in the field of regional California verse: Sterling, Miss French, Clark Ashton Smith. I speak of this area as it existed before hard-boiled professional invaders like Jeffers, Winters, and Rexroth invaded its backyard Pacific Coast culture and professionalized it. The golden sunlight of suburban, pre-smog, pre-sound-film California plays over Mr. Fryer's text.

Now for *Songs and Sonnets Atlantean:* Mr. Fryer purports to write a sequence of descriptive poems not about Plato's Atlantis but about a 13,000 B.C. Atlantean kingdom out beyond Gibraltar in "our" Atlantic Ocean. This ocean had the bad taste to flood the kingdom over and leave only a few upthrusting seamarks (the Canaries, the Mariettas and Cape Verde Islands) as memorials to a 10-island kingdom [i.e., empire] stretching between Africa and the Americas. I confess I read this Herodotean history as an infidel until I reached pp. 120-121, the long footnote to Sonnet V, "Atkantharia." Here I learned that this colonial empire was built on a huge pomegranate trade (wines, inks, dyes, cosmetics) produced from an equally huge pomegranate. The seed-pulps ran as large as our decadent modern cherries. As a true pomegranater, I was immediately converted, and threw away the technical *Fortune*-mag. notes I'd taken, querying the trade sources that justified the huge ports described on p. 119, for instance.

But as far as Mr. Fryer himself is concerned—remember his photo on the back cover?—*Songs and Sonnets Atlantean* only uses Atlantis for subject matter; the book is really a tribute to the Elizabethan (I) Edmund Spenser. Mr. Fryer considers himself an analogous Elizabethan (II) poet in style and content, with Atlantis equivalent to the Camelot of Spenser's *Faerie Queene.* For his key sonnet sequence (I-XVII, pp. 78–94), Mr. Fryer has expanded FQ's famous stanza form to create a new type of "sonnet:" stanzaed 9-3-2, rhymed ABABBCBCC-DCD-EE; metered lines 1-8 iambic (x/); lines 9-14 seven or six-foot iambic, depending on some private Elizabethan code. What is Sterling-Californian, not Spenser-English, is Mr. Fryer's refusal to devise an Atlantean story-poem like Spenser's Arthurian *Queene*. Mr. Fryer has the "modern" (post-Wordsworth) belief in descriptive landscape poetry. Spenser took more interest in telling verse-stories or in the psychological arguments of his Platonic hymns and of his sonnet sequence, "Amoretti."

Mr. Fryer has nothing to say in his poems. This is reflected in the deflating form of his sonnets: 9-3-2. Both the orthodox English patterns make the conclusion structurally more important, whether in the octet argument of 8-6 or in the snapper-couplet of 4-4-4-2. (Mr. Fryer's couplet-conclusions are more relaxed and metrically longer.) The strict prose sense in Mr. Fryer's poems is banal. What he wishes, is of course the mellifluousness of the Surrey tradition in Elizabethan (I) poetry, to which Spenser and Marlowe contributed and to which contemporary poets like [St. John] Perse, Stevens and Hart Crane still belong.

But the sonnet was invented as a form, back in Italy, not so much for pretty writing, but to express difficulties and tensions. It wasn't a technically demanding form in Italian, no matter what American high school teachers say about it now. Compared to its source form, the difficult sestina, sonnets are almost free verse. The interesting English sonnets grew not from the Surrey tradition but from Sir Thomas Wyatt (–Sidney–Donne–the dramatist Shakespeare), and many of these sonneteers were considered metrically rough, coarse writers. Historically, there has always been some famous poet in English who could turn out a good example of the form, but it is perhaps significant that since Milton the greatest technicians (Pope, Tennyson, Eliot) have been bored by the form. Mr. Fryer must be the only poet to have listened to *Green Sleeves* (p. 67)—OK, Vaughan Williams' *Fantasia*—and not try to write words that fit the melody. To write in the sonnet form about *Green Sleeves* suggests a coarse ear.

Bibliographers of Fritz Leiber will note his tributary "Secretest" (p. 97).

(The text of Mr. Purcell's review has been reproduced from its reappearance in *Nyctalops* Nos. 11-12 [April 1976].)

Ends & Odds

A Poetic Miscellany

In Verse and Prose

DEDICATED
TO WADE GERMAN,

*fellow poet and craftsman,
with affection and high regard.*

Contents

St. Ichabod	127
The Conquistadors	128
A Modest Breviary	129
A Labyrinth of Caverns	130
Swimming Somewhere in the Antillias	131
A Modest Beastiary	132
A Colonnade out of Time	133
Temporal Enigma	134
On the Death Mask of J. Sheridan Le Fanu	135
The Crippled Octopus	136
To a Professor of Professors	137
Puzzlement	138
Isca Silurum	139
The Capricorn	140
The Key	141
Brave Ocean Cavaliers	142
Queen Elizabeth II: 2016	143
What's in a Name? Indeed, Just What Lies in a Name?	144
Where Now the Towns of Legend and of Myth?	146
And Have You Seen a Peacock as of Late?	147
Retrospective	148
Have You Viewed the Big Five? Are They All still Extant?	149
Enigma	154
The Bird of Indigo and Verde	155
The Transcendence of King Bhumibol	156
"Yea, Though I Walk through the Valley of the Numen of Light. . . ."	157
Another Forsaken Garden	158
The Forsaken Garden Again	159
Some Holy Grail	161
Another Grail Re-found	162

An Obvious Announcement	163
Artorius, Arthurius, or Arthur Rex?	164
The Lyre-Bird	165
Upon a Maya Pyramid in El Salvador	166
The Nonsense Eater	167
A King out of Macedonia	169
Alexandros Megalos	170
Fountains	171
Katnyptian	172
A Song in Reverse	173
A Sunday Noontide Ritual	174
Mouse in Boots	176
The "X"–The Unknown Quantity	177
By the Light of Flambeaux	178
The Grove of Ceiba Trees along the Stream	179
Those Giant Ceiba Trees Again	180
From Script to Script, From Crypt to Crypt	181
On Jesse Allen's Biggest African Tableau	182
"The Girl with the Ice Cream Tits"	183
The New Conquistadors	184
Lo Ordinario	185
A Maya Pyramid Revisited	186
The Cup from Otherwhere	187
Divertissement I	188
Divertissement II	189
Transition	191
To H. P. L.–A Tribute out of Time	192
A Bit of Nostalgia	193
The Hunting of the Ampersand	194
Notes, *by Dlanod Yendis*	203

Ends and Odds

St. Ichabod

St. Ichabod the cat lay prone upon the couch—
Whether he merely slept, whether he calmly sat,
He had such dignity, he clearly was no slouch.

At forty pounds, was he a mini jungle cat,
Or like a lynx, but big and broad, and yet not fat,
A huge domestic cat with rare ancestral kinks?

He lived an ideal life, such as "Where it was at."—
Was he not equal to a somewhat larger lynx,
As if perhaps descended from some grand Egyptian sphinx?

Serene and confident, he was a great big cat,
A big black cat, black as the blackest of black inks—
Loved by Bastet, he had become a pampered brat.

But still he charmed, and with his black and glossy fur
He lived a better life as *him,* less harshly than as *her.*

Friday, 30th October 2015.

The Conquistadors

Translated from the French of José-Maria de Heredia.

Like a flight of falcons out of their native charnel,
Wearied of carrying their proud, vain poverty,
From Palos de Moguer, captains and veteran sailors
Depart, drunk with a dream heroical and brutal.

They have gone to obtain the legendary metal
That Cipango matures in her mines faraway,
And the gentle trade-winds have inclined their antennas
Toward the mysterious coasts of the far western world.

Each evening they hope for some epic tomorrows:
The phosphorescent azure of the Tropical Seas
Entrances their sleep with a golden-hued mirage;

When, leaning at the prows on their white caravelles,
They behold where lift up, against an unknown sky,
From out the Ocean's depths the unfamiliar stars.

Sunday, 1 November 2015.

A Modest Breviary

Just a few modest prayers to honor Mother Nature,
For she pins all her hopes on us as the one species,
Since we seem to absorb all the rest with erasure:

Awesome burden for her and for us, with our p.c.'s,
And for our ever-swelling tide of town-made feces,
Which we might better utilize for our food crops:

The random killing-off of all the other species
On behalf of our own as the top of the tops?—
For all the other life can only we command the stops?

Dear Mother God, protect us, and all other life,
Against ourselves, for if indeed we are the tops,
Nothing is exempt from our carelessness and strife!

Awesome burden, indeed, as if we possibly could care
For anything beyond our kind, by so much as a hair!

Wednesday, 4 November 2015.

A Labyrinth of Caverns

The mound: you enter from the top, to find
The labyrinth of caverns underneath,
Where most of them connect, but some are blind:
How different from the plain, the open heath,
Those vast, enshadowed caverns underneath,
Which lead to yet another underground:
One level to another still beneath,
Aye downward to the last and inmost bound,
To where the planet's rock enfolds the molten core around:

Without that star-fire thus entombed, and old beyond belief,
While safe inside our space-suit skins, while rational and sound,
We could not face our cosmic quest with joy or with relief:

The star-fire still inside us, what implanted it, and why?—
    To make us to seek it, to find it, to explore,
    Perhaps by means of cryptic gate, of cosmic door,
Illumined by the star-fire beacons fixed throughout the sky?

Friday, 20 November 2015.

Swimming Somewhere in the Antillias

Translated from "Ancestral memory."

From where we sat around that larger cove,
We spied an underwater wonder-sphere
Into whose ultragorgeous depths we dove:
Coral and giant shells rose here and there,
And flame-bright fishes flashed afar and near,
Too glamorous to tempt our appetite:
Rejoiced, we swam beyond all fright or fear,
Discovering delights as well we might,
Inside a weightless world of water, shade, and light:

We must have sojourned there, in Greatermost Antillia,
Where some yet mythoglyphic script the tide and sand indite,
North of the site of lost, subsided Atlantillia:

The biting sadness that we felt, from that majestic loss,
Soon disappeared . . . beneath our moment's beauty with its gloss.

Thursday, 26 November 2015.

A Modest Beastiary

Yes, beas-ti-ar-y, not bes-ti-ar-y,
And yes, please note, you have perused it right,
As beas-tee-air-ee, not bess-chee-air-ee:
To notice, one need not be very bright!
Like a good fish, you have preferred to bite;
I compliment you on that wise decision,
Even as you tell me, to go fly a kite,
That you know that I'm open to derision,
Like someone caught amid an adult circumcision.

What is this modest *bestiaire?* Just little animals,
Like daddy longlegs, flies or fleas, bugs almost beyond vision,
And tiny things that feast on us like tiny cannibals.

However flimsy or despised, these varmints have their charms;
They too deserve some special thought, perhaps a coat of arms.

Monday, 7 December 2015.

A Colonnade out of Time

The Roman soldiers digging in the sand,
South of the Ocean-Gates of Hercules,
Had found some fragment from an elder land;
Out of the dunes, appearing by degrees,
A colonnade emerged—it seemed to please
By its exotic pillars with volutes:
Unlike the stone of some antiquities,
This rock withstood their legionary boots—
It had withstood far greater force than what came with these brutes:

When earthquake and tsunami had engulfed it all in sand,
Sucked up from the seafloor, the seamounts, and the ocean-buttes,
And hurled in one huge wave of waves down on this inner land;

The soldiers left; they thought they might return; they never did.
The waves of sand engulfed it back, once more securely hid.

Thursday, 17 December 2015.

Temporal Enigma

It was an ancient building from the future,
But quite how old, we could not justly gauge
At something subtle as a seam or suture,—
At anything so transient as is age,
Like measuring the magnitude of rage—
The future might wax older than the past:
The creviced seam or suture, like a cage,
Like land enshadowed by an overcast,
Grips all the time-and-season zones, as does the Vast:

If it exists as one grand seam or suture
That weaves all things as one both tight and fast,
Then Time controls the present, past, and future:

That ancient building from the future seemed to grow
    Newer and younger every day—how lyrical!—
    In substance and in style until—a miracle—
It looked more like the future as envisioned long ago.

Saturn-day, 16 January 2016.

On the Death Mask of J. Sheridan Le Fanu

(For Brian J. Showers.)

Was he so debonair this author who,
Grasping the crafty supernatural,
Became *the* J. Sheridan Le Fanu?
How he revealed the more than natural!
And more, *beyond* the hypernatural,
Subtleties that make you doubt your own mind!—
Until you shout out, "Holy Mackerel,
It's darker than I thought!" It's what I find
Unseen above me, to the side, before me and behind!

And that is what, unseen but *felt,* that turns me pale with fright,
That makes me frantic, makes me lose my balance and my mind,
The Presences Invisible that rule by day, by night!

The green tea that he sold me in that shop!—but from which tin?
(Do only I perceive this imp, who greets me like his kin?)

Moon-day, late afternoon, 18 January 2016.

The Crippled Octopus

(A parody of *Cephalopod in Residence*.)

The crippled octopus or squid or squidlet,
To function, needs more than one tentacle,
Plus intuition, or plus id or idlet,—
As when a sudden murmur in the auricle,
Or something like it in the ventricle,
Can serve as well as any prophecy
Or premonition—from an oracle,
To warn him well, and with efficacy,
That something might be wrong, or off, officially.

So, get him to an octopodal prosthetist? No, wait—
How Mother Nature operates! not superficially—
I had forgot: his lost or damaged arms regenerate!

He has therefore—far more than just utilitarian—
No need to seek a submarine veterinarian.

Saturn-day, 25 March 2016.

To a Professor of Professors

(For Judd Hubert.)

> Your breath stays with me:
> poetry is the only cure
> for the disease of life
> poetry is the light
> that is never lost
> poetry is the soul's
>   chemotherapy.
>   –Jack Foley,
>   "An Incantation for
> Francisco X. Alarcón in His Illness."

Thank you, dear friend and mentor, for the lore,
The love of language and literature,
The lamp, the lantern, needed to explore—
As passionate as any thurifer
Who chants, processioning for Jupiter,
Or Lucifer—might they not be the same?
Between Prometheus and Lucifer,
Both bringing light or fire—which one to blame,
Or praise, the more?—since each one fits inside that very frame;

And like the twain of them the teacher brings both light and fire,
The passing of a sacral fire that learning must inflame—
The teacher has a hero's task, to teach and to inspire:

Once more has one transcended back, back to the Other Side,
To some retreat, between the lives, to sojourn or abide?

Saturn-day, noontide, 2 April 2016.

Puzzlement

Historiography, or history—
Might that be better than a chronicle?—
That some think so, remains a mystery:
But any memoir is a miracle
Preserved in some form safe and physical,
Then hidden, that is, buried in the ground;
Better than by some writ historical,
So does an object serve, concrete and sound,
As when a metal Capricorn in Caer Leon is found:

That sign, the standard of the Second, or Augustan, Legion,
Can work as well as any writ for that which we propound,
A single object best illumes a single place or region:

Whether by object or by writ, howevermuch perplexed,
All things phenomenal of every type may serve as text.

Freya's day, late afternoon, 8 April 2016.

Isca Silurum

Usk-Town of the Silurians

(For Arthur Machen as Leolinus Siluriensis.)

The Capricorn, the bottom half a fish,
The upper half, a two-horned bearded goat,
Apt emblem on a standard or a dish:
A proper figurehead for ship or boat,
For any grandiosity afloat,
A giant barge carved for an emperor:
Athletic soldier or a slob with bloat,
Thus up the Usk as princely traveller,
The great man soon will pace inside the amphitheatre:

Amid the pomp and splendor, here where this is no museum,
When in the arena's games and sports, he plays the arbiter,
An echo far from Mother Rome and from her Colosseum:

Newport encroaches from the south;
    These hanging wooded hills confirm
    That Caer Leon on Usk stands firm,
As much as time or space alloweth.

Saturn-day, noontide, 9 April 2016.

The Capricorn

That ancient sign or symbol did not point
Before or after, only to the side—
The divagation did not disappoint:
With naught but gloom or darkness as our guide,
The invitation had in truth not lied,
Where we turned left inside that darkling wood:
How marvellous that we had veered aside,
Albeit that it promised naught of good,
Naught but that overcast and cryptic neighborhood;

And yet how glamourous those darkling trees appeared,
Far more alluring than some sun-bedazzled wood,
Alive with shapes half-seen, mysterious, and weird:

Beyond that wood, a glade; beyond that glade, another wood;
Creating more phantastick shapes, as well that forest could.

Thursday afternoon, 21 April 2016.

The Key

The key seemed ancient, but it bore no tarnish;
Hard as iron, but more like pale flame-gold,
Ungalvanized, no varathane, no varnish:
Its big, ungainly shape—what lock could hold
That awkward key?—which held a certain cold,
A certain chill, that could not be denied;
As we watch Nature's narrative unfold,
We learn, as those who find, or who have tried,
This truth—a key can open, but it cannot guide:

And thus it turned out in this case. We had the key,
But where then was the lock? Hidden, where all has died
For centuries? Where was that lock? On land or sea?

The problem lay beyond resolve, and beyond measure,
Something that mocked our search, our quest—ironic treasure.

Sunday morning, 1 May 2016.

Brave Ocean Cavaliers

Intrepid surfer dudes who rule the waves like knights,
Who ride the wild and white-maned horses of the deep,
Where winds and waves combine, to rise, to fall, to leap,
Dancing in that mélange of plumes and frothing heights:

Feel how the piquant salt within the ocean bites,
Refreshing soul and sense where waters whirl and heap,
Before the breaking wave, that wave so tall and steep,
Arrives ashore, while dazzling with its wall of lights.

How brief this apotheosis of soul and sea,
When Mother Ocean Sea holds on, then lets us go;
Sublime the bliss, the high, but far too transitory:

Too brief, too much like Love's own height, or it might be—
Amid the Forum's moil, its endless amphigory—
A sudden lightning bolt, compelling a mortal "Oh!"

Wednesday morning, 25 May 2016.

Queen Elizabeth II: 2016

(Born 1926—regnant since 1952.)

We have her image on a piece of Royal Mail
Included in a letter from a British friend—
We cannot help but pause, to ponder, to reflect.

The photo that we note, from shoulders to her hat,
Equates with more or less a standard sculptured bust—
An understated elegance predominates.

She wears a wide-brimmed hat, with a small cake-shaped cap;
A modest, but becoming, formal suit-dress outfit;
Three strings of pearls around her neck, and with pearls at her ears.

For once we do not see her handbag, or her purse;
Her teeth gleam as well as her pearls, they seem to match,
But best of all her smile appears content and glorious.

Whereas Victoria deceased at eighty-two;
    Elizabeth, at ninety, still seems fresh and young.
    A gracious alchemy hath worked its magick here:
No need to rule, they each have reigned a full sixty-four years.

Thursday evening, 26 May 2016.

What's in a Name?
Indeed, Just What Lies in a Name?

Messrs. Marco Polo of Venice and Rustichello of Pisa,
The Description of the World, begun about 1298 A.D.

(For Robert W. Thompson and E. Sandra Morgan.)

What's in a name? I ask you, Messer Marco Polo!
Or for that matter then—if it is not all play—
What's in a tale? I ask you, Messer Rustichello!

Words, phrases, sentences: the building blocks of language:
Status unknown or undecided, in suspense.

Master Marco Polo, do tell the other half
That you left undescribed, untold, unheralded,
In your great opus, *The Description of the World:*
Your truth is far more fabulous than any fiction!

Master Rustichello, declare yourself at once,
Much more than fabulist, a true mythographer—
That's why *he* asked your help, in writing down his memoirs,
No mere redaction, but sublime hyperbole!

Do tell what might lurk hidden in a given name—
What wonders or what marvels, in a given tale.
From Rex Artorius, King Arthur otherwise,
To China's Kublai Khan, or Venice's own son—
From Camelot to Khanbalikh to Cambaluc?
From China or Cathay, Sri Lanka or Ceylon,
Cipango or Japan, to Java or Sumatra?
From Mother India to Hindustan and Ind?
Or from the Moluccas to the Andaman Islands?

What's in a name like cinnabar that comes through trade?
From cenobre and zinjafr to zinjifrah,
From red mercuric sulfide, or bright yellow-red,

The only ore of mercury of real import?
Likewise a little worm that yields the selfsame dye,
Vermeil from vermicule—vermilion otherwise?
From candy bar and cinnabar to Zanzibar?

Just what lies in a name, O Messer Marco Polo?
Or for that matter then—if it is not all play—
Just what lies in a tale, O Messer Rustichello?

Created several years before 2015-16-17.

Where Now the Towns of Legend and of Myth?

> In Xanadu did Kubla Khan
> A stately pleasure-dome decree:
> —Samuel Taylor Coleridge, "Kubla Khan."

Some forty leagues away due northeast of Tatu,
Whether at Shangtu, Chengde, Xamdu, or Xanadu
(Whichever name a captious expert might prefer),
Did Kubilai Khan command a lavish hunting lodge?—
But not as lavish quite as that Forbidden City
Nestled within Tatu, which we now call Beijing,
Elsewise the Khanbaliq or Cambaluc of legend,
The northern capital of Khitai or Cathay—
Or did he but rebuild or renovate that fortressed lodge?

No matter: To a poet it became a pleasure-dome,
A house or domus, more a stately mansion, or a church,
A temple, or cathedral, coruscating to the sky:

Native or non-native, today the tourists come
To view the place that still remains the hunting lodge.

Sunday afternoon, 14 August 2016.

And Have You Seen a Peacock as of Late?

> What cosmic jewelsmith could have designed this bird,
> His body and his tail, his crest and outspread fan?
> —D. Sidney-Fryer, "The Bird of Indigo and Verde."

And have you seen a peacock as of late?—
Trailing afar his long and massive tail—
His passing-by is more than worth the wait!
He glides near smooth and stately as a snail,
His beauty dominates, however frail,
And yet the tail conceals his modest queue:
Kaleidoscope that none might countervail,
As when his fan spreads out, all praise falls due—
It turns into a monstrance but of green and gold and blue.

As if his plumage could perform as coat of mail,
As if a giant cat might stop, and stare askew,
As if such wonderment would make a wild beast quail?

Such gorgeousness, such glamour, and on such a scale,
    Albeit fabled, they demand no quest;
Such startling beauty quite lives on outside the pale,
    This maharajah bird with plumuled crest.

Saturday noon, 3 September 2016.

Retrospective

I have lived long enough to become an old man,
I who thought I would not live to turn twenty-one.
Might I still recollect back to when I began?
Eighty-two times have I now gone around the sun,
While with our planet's orb and orbit being one,
As part of some unknown but all-pervasive mind.
Where was the self before this last life had begun?—
Like a new life with yet an older life combined,
Like a new vine with yet an older vine utterly entwined?

To seek the treasures of the mind, and of the inner self,
To seek the dazzling treasure-troves of Hindustan, of Ynd:
Which one is worth the more, the inner life, the outer pelf?

The treasures of the arts live on,
    but can the artist still survive?
To play his all-potential role,
    he must somehow remain alive.

Sunday evening, 18 September 2016.

Have You Viewed the Big Five? Are They All still Extant?

(*Adagio lamentoso.*)

Have you viewed the Big Five? Are they all still extant?
Where have you gone in Africa? Desert or jungle?
The forested terrain of Central Africa?
That's a great choice! But let me repeat my first question;
Have you seen the Big Five? Are they all still alive?
Lion, giraffe, rhinoceros, and elephant?
The hippopotamus? What other pachyderms?
Have you lain like a lamb with your back to a lion?
Have you shared a carafe of wine with a giraffe?
Have you run on the veldt with a rhinoceros?
Have you sat on the grass next to an elephant?
Did he let you approach, and kiss him on the nose,
On the trunk that serves him like a strong and lithe arm?
Like an almighty arm that can move like a crane?
Have you swum in a lake with a hippopotamus?

Don't ask me. I am at best just a traveller,
Just passing through, in at one door, out at another;
No expert. Ask instead the Question Answer Man!

(Have you viewed the Big Five? Are they all still extant?)
Thanks for your sage advice, but before I might heed it,
I must make sure to remember these other questions:
A kind of little list, to cover all the issues.
What of the other animals? Who speaks for them?
What fabled beasts and birds? What of their habitats?
What of the golden Indic tiger with black stripes?
What of the snow-pale tiger of Siberia?—
The one and only tiger of the ice and snow—
Impalpable against the cold and wintry land,
White with pale stripes, near soundless, near invisible!

But bigger than them all, what of the elephant?—
The lion is but one king, the elephant the chief one.
What of the birds and beasts of legend and of fable?

(Have you seen the Big Five? Are they all still alive?)
Let me repeat, me as the lowly traveller:
Apparently you have a plethora of questions.
Address them to the Question Answer Man himself.
(The Question Answer Man? Who on earth could that be?)

The name is Gruen, but written Grune, and rimed with tune;
The full name is Roald Grune, the last name means but Green,
The greatest eco-hero-journalist of all!
(Yes, who could be this Mister Grune, the Answer Man?)

(Has he viewed the Big Five? Are they all still extant?)
He was, he is, he always will be Mister Green.
Yes, after due research on my p.c., I find him:
Our newsman on the ground, in the air, on the water,
Under the sea, in outer or in inner space,
Travelling by hot-air balloon, by train, by tank,
By aëroplane, automobile, or submarine,
By dugout or canoe, by any sailing ship,
By rocket ship, by ether ship, or space-craft otherwise.
He monitors the species moribund, or dead;
Vanishing, or vanished, they have no choice at all,
With us or against us they have no chance at all,
They have no choice or chance, except to disappear.
What of the birds and beasts of legend and of myth?
Let me repeat my questions on them and their habitats.

(If you don't care about the living and their kind,
Why would you care concerning those we cannot see?—
Never you mind the beasts and birds of myth and fable.)

(Has he seen the Big Five? Are they all still alive?)
A dialogue delayed, *the* Mister Green will now respond,
Discovered in the middle of a lecture hall.

* * *

Thank you, Professor Grune, for your attention and response.
(Thank you, Sir, for your intelligent list of questions.)
I have perused them all, and here is my response.
I have seen the Big Five, and all the other animals:
Some have gone; some are going; some are still hanging on.
I have travelled the globe, and circled it in space.
Apart from the species that we grow for our table,
For their meat, for their milk, for their wool and whatever,
We need not fret concerning our farm animals:
We make sure that they continue just as before.

(Have we seen the Big Five? Are they all still alive?)
Let me address your list, but take it in reverse.
We need not fret about the camel-leöpard—
If indeed he is not the same as the giraffe—
Nor yet the unicorn, nor any suchlike creatures:
They disappeared, and long ago, for other worlds.
As for the walrus, and for the elephant seal,
No less the other seals, they manage to hold on;
Ditto for the musk-ox, and for the caribou.
The tiger of the snows, that of Siberia,
Luckily so remote, also somehow survives.
The Indic tiger, safe in special forest parks,
Is otherwise extant, by the skin of his teeth;
The Florida panther?—he still roams the Everglades.
The tiger-jaguär in tropical America
Has just sufficient jungle to conceal himself.

(Have you viewed the Big Five? Are they all still extant?)
The lion, the giraffe, and the rhinoceros,
No less the hippopotamus: they manage to hold on.
As for the Afro pachyderm, it's touch and go,
Never you mind his tusks, that fatal ivory.
But, as the larger landscape that he must traverse
For forage, for water, as well as for his graveyard,
Keeps on shrinking, it is but a matter of time
Before his numbers also keep diminishing:
He, too, shall vanish back into the primal nothing.

* * *

However, on the other hand, the Asian elephant
Bids fair to carry on. His tusks are not esteemed
As a source of ideal ivory to be carved.
And what is more, he has use industrially;
Both strong and well-behaved, he can move, and perform
Where machines—bulldozers, and backhoes, and big cranes—
Cannot go, cannot operate, and simply will not do.
The beasts need food and water, and they need more care;
They must be bathed and washed, but their kind and wise handler
Gains a friend, no less a companion, all in one—
So much more, so much better, than a mere machine.

(Yes, please don't ask again that question, not right here.)
And we have not so much as touched upon the oceans,
The cetaceans, the cephalopods, and all the many fishes.
The cetaceans teeter still upon extinction:
The dolphins and the porpoises, they seem okay,
But the big whales of every type are in real trouble,
Never you mind the trash and filth we vomit in the sea,
Whether from our settlements, or from our many ships.
Now the cephalopods, the squids and octopi,
Overall they appear to be doing much better
Than the overhunted cetaceans, the big whales.
But think! We have reduced the fishes that we eat
Down to their lowest levels in these modern times.
We should at least allow them to regenerate;
Otherwise they will vanish in their turn as well,
An awesome and mindboggling process of extinction!

(We have seen the Big Five, they are all still extant.)
As Julian Huxley made so bold to prophesy
Back in the summertime of Nineteen Hundred Fifty-Five,
In print, in the *Scientific American,*
In an article entitled "World Population," thus:
As the sheer mass of human flesh keeps on increasing,
The flesh of all the other species will decrease,
Except for the insects, and our farm animals:

And all the rest will mostly vanish into nothing.
(Yes, possibly they might deserve a better fate than that.)
Prosperity for humans only hastens this whole process
Of destruction, or extinction, or extermination.

(We have seen the Big Five, and all the other animals.)
The problem lies with us ourselves: *too many people.*
(Too many people? but—but how can people stop
From making love, and making babies, in their turn?)
Is it not alarming, or am I too alarmist?
Am I political, or too political?
Am I polemical, or too polemical?
In short, in sum, there simply are too many people.
That's my response to all your enquiries of doom,
Ghastly and grim, both bleak and bare, and with no quibbling.

Whether for us or all the other species on the planet,
There shall not be a mass escape on into the stars,
An exodus in some vast fleet of rocket ships.
We, and only we, can engineer our own destruction,
As well as that of all the other non-plant life,
Through our own procreation, uncontrollable.
If we can't manage here, how could we manage otherwhere?!
That's my response, that's my advice. Take it or leave it.
So, go view the Big Five, while they still are alive.

(This list could be diminished or extended, either way.)

Friday evening, 30 September 2016

Enigma

That ancient Roman villa must have passed
Through much rebuilding on a major scale
To last this long, or longer, at long last.
Built solid to withstand the ocean's gale,
It had withstood the weather without fail,
Intact, two thousand years, above those waves
Too rough or turbulent for any sail—
The villa stands with walls and architraves
Upon its lonely bluff where strong wind rants and raves.

An ancient palace worthy of an emperor,
An empty shell whereon the rainfall pours, and laves
The blighted gardens . . . cursed by sphinx or sorcerer?

What infamous or famous family might
    have once resided in this house?
Where nothing now inhabits or resides,
    nor wee small bird, nor wee small mouse.

Monday morning, 3 October 2016.

The Bird of Indigo and Verde

What cosmic jewelsmith could have designed this bird,
His body and his tail, his crest and outspread fan?
His tail, such overkill, could not seem more absurd,
But he, like all of us, must heed the goad of Pan
Amalgamate of gold, of azurine and verde,
No greater jewellery since time on Earth began!

Friday morning, 7 October 2016

The Transcendence of King Bhumibol

(Bhumibol Adulyadej, 1928-2016.)

The king of Thailand has at last deceased,
After years of ill health, of slow decline,
All while his virtue otherwise increased:
A good king, he did good, and by design,
For folk across the land, an honest sign
Of rectitude, in person best applied:
Such kindness, more than decent, is divine,
Partaking of a grandeur—bonafide,
Magnanimous, celestial—of nirvana magnified:

Yes, after so much evil otherwhere and otherwise,
Let us acclaim the good, no less than as personified—
In great king Bhumibol—the kind, compassionate, and wise:

A nation's anthem has he made, sung on the saxophone,
Exchanging with Duke Ellington some jazzy polytone.

Sunday morning, 22 October 2016.

"Yea, Though I Walk through the Valley of the Numen of Light. . . ."

With easy lush-green slopes on either side
It lay, that lovely valley, straight ahead,
Amid whose contours one could gently glide:
With giant roses of empurpled red,
Great banks of rosebush-trees had shed, had bled,
Enormous drifts of petals as of snow:
Like drops of blood they pass to brown from red,
Dark metamorphosis, from tip to toe—
Then by fierce autumn rains and winds, thrown to and fro:

The day stayed bright and clear, as we proceeded on,
On. through that lovely valley, free from threat or foe,
Until we reached the wood, the furthest we had gone:

Reluctantly we turned around, to head back home;
We had exhausted, for that day, our wish to roam.

Sunday afternoon, 23 October 2016.

Another Forsaken Garden

She idly wandered on behind the manse,
On into the neglected garden space,
While noticing the toil of bees and ants:
Oblivious of her form, her gown, her face,
The insects toiled on, each in its own place,
While she stood near the ornamental urn:
Upon its plinth, at the top of the vase,
The cone-shaped cap, she clearly could discern,
Transformed on into a tridented crown in its own turn:

Ancient Atlantis once again? So, how did *that* get here?
Who could have made or found it? Whom to ask? From whom to learn?
Too easily such knowledge often seems to disappear.

She studied the exotic urn, amused, amazed, bemused—
This crown and trident *here,* how often used and then re-used?

Tuesday afternoon, 25 October 2016.

The Forsaken Garden Again

After several years she had returned to the old manse. Her dear aunt and uncle had both deceased, quickly, no suffering, the aunt first and then the uncle. Their daughter and son had inherited the property, plus a more than adequate sum of money, not only to maintain themselves, but the property no less, in particular the large-scale manse and the various outbuildings. Almost at once, house and grounds had received much attention and refurbishment. With their own beginning families the daughter and son had elected to live on in the manse—after an absence of several years while they had attended college, and had begun their own professional lives, the daughter a dentist, and the son a doctor, both ministering to the local country population. They had invited her, their somewhat older cousin, still unattached, to come visit for a while, and maybe even to live there if she so desired. As a freelance writer and poet, she could reside anywhere. So, why not live with her cousins on a trial basis?

Some fashionable and expensive architect in New York City had designed all the buildings on the property during the later 1800s. Her aunt and uncle had specified a substantial Tudor-style main house with matching stables, a caretaker couple's residence, a gatehouse, and so forth. The architect had more than satisfied their wish, and had even innovated something special for the main house. Extending over an outsized level space like a low plateau, the mansion, or palace, had three or four main wings, each one with subsidiary wings, along with pitched roofs, many gables, and many chimneys. The architect had adroitly made the whole group of interconnected structures to resemble from a distance not just a village but a village of great houses. The solid stone foundations and lower walls, the dark-stained beams and the off-white plaster of the upper walls and gables, all stood out handsomely, not less the many mullioned windows or window bays.

The entire complex of buildings had cost a small fortune in and of itself. However, it had hardly made a dent in the considerable combined income of both aunt and uncle, based solidly on inherited railroad fortunes, carefully maintained and administered. They had had the entire complex of edifices constructed on a high and quite extensive peninsula with rock-bound shores extending out into the ocean from southeastern Massachusetts, rather like an annex of the lordly properties gathered in and around Newport, Rhode Island, further to the west, but relatively nearby.

This then was the manse to which the daughter and son in their own turn had invited their somewhat older cousin, who in addition to her talent as a novelist or poet had become celebrated as a great beauty. Withal she had remained a kind, sweet, pleasant person, one who had steadfastly resisted marriage to date, although she now found her defences ineluctably crumbling.

Soon after her arrival back at the old manse, designed to look even older than what it was, she went out into the once inexplicably forsaken garden space just behind the principal wing of the gigantic house. Her face registered astonishment! The gardeners had trimmed and pruned the trees and bushes, cleared out the detritus, the dead limbs and accumulated leaves. They had cleaned and redone the graveled walks, no less than the fountains here and there, unobtrusively purling and re-purling. She went up to that certain ornamental urn upon its plinth, and looked at it keenly. Someone, perhaps a gardener, had cleaned both plinth and urn, and had repaired several small cracks and fissures here and there. And a metalsmith with great care had likewise cleaned the crown and trident, and then varnished it, so that the metal—no less than that orichalch mentioned by Plato and other ancient writers—now shone forth with all the pristine beauty of the original pale flame-gold, of silver and gold and copper cunningly intermixed. She sighed a deep sigh, and felt a profound sense of aesthetic satisfaction. But the mystery remained, more unfathomable than ever.

Saturn-day morning, 29 October 2016.

Some Holy Grail

Upon a summer's evening broad and warm,
When calm and quiet lay among the trees,
I seemed to note, half glimpsed, a shining form:
Somewhere amid this world's interstices,
It somewhat waxed, and brightened, by degrees,
A cup, a goblet, or a modest pail:
Therein, what might have settled as the lees?
The object for a quest, for good, for bale—
Equivocal—Satanic chalice, or celestial grail?—

What if it happened that amid all those resplendent knights
Some there were who searched for a darker wine, a darker ale,
Such as preferred by Lucifer ere cast from Heaven's lights?

All quests can function equally for evil as for good,
As with those grim auxiliaries of would, of should, of could.

Tuesday evening, 1 November 2016.

Another Grail Re-found

Next day at dawn, while on my solo walk
From farmhouse to the neighboring estate,
I revelled in the change from idle talk:
But something lured me on—was it innate?—
Like last night's radiant cup—or was that fate?—
Or visible horizon to the east?
How light I felt, as if I had no weight,
And keenly searched where night at last had ceased,
While I stood watch in silence as the sun's own rays increased:

Along the paved and private road, where trees yet cast much shade,
I searched ahead the sky, the land, where night had now surceased,
While I stood still in wonderment, and utterly afraid:

But fear soon changed to joy when I perceived the sun's wide cup,
And peered adown inside that grail while also looking up!

Wednesday morning, 2 November 2016.

An Obvious Announcement

Dear reader, you are surely not a fool:
You have quite rightly figured it all out,
That as a poet I remain Old School.
A something certain in an age of doubt,
A constant fountain in a time of drought,
My lineage I state, and have no shame,
While such a term still carries weight and clout,
A modern arch-romantic without blame—
My heritage—why not flaunt it, instead of mock or flout?

To wit, all fantasy at least, and all imagination,
As undergone by hominids, take place where they come out,
Out from their locus or their geographical location.

The time, the space, the planet, all possess an equal weight
Determining the entity, its choices, or its fate.

Monday morning, 7 November 2016.

Artorius, Arthurius, or Arthur Rex?

As mounted cataphractarius chief,
Or perhaps even more, as king, or kyning,
Did he but lead, then hold estates in fief?
As dux bellorum, seeming always winning,
He ever led the armies on his inning,
His turn at power, across a varied clime—
The clash of arms and armor ever dinning,
Still deafening, across the waste of time,
And this was when the world still seemed pristine and fresh and
    prime.

With echoes that ring on and on, however thin and thinning,
The cosmos yet maintains its pulse, its rhythm and its rime,
Kaleidoscope of sound and sight that keeps the head a-spinning.

When by an empire's vanished sun, then and thereafter litten,
Was he that Rhiothamus who ruled Brittany and Britain?

Monday evening, 7 November 2016.

The Lyre-Bird

Item: the triple species of the lyre-bird.

A fact: that Nature features odd coincidence,
And more often than not, an avian excellence.
    Three "ornithos" of Oz
    Exist against the odds,
The laws of probability and consequence.

Though not as lordly as the peacock, it may hap,
The lyre-bird's tail might happen, or indeed might hap,
    To warrant serious attention—
    Its music still goes without mention:
The wind that whispers through its lyre, a subtle gap.

Even without some six or seven strings of wire,
The lyre-bird still somehow makes music through his lyre.
    Though this is not his modest song,
    As when his fan spreads out—for how long?—
The music it creates goes into its own gyre.

Tuesday morning, 8 November 2016.

Upon a Maya Pyramid in El Salvador

> Let us deal gently with our dead illusions, in
> the hope that they will also deal gently with us.
> —Clark Ashton Smith,
> "Epigrams and Apothegms," *Spells and Philtres.*

(For Ignatius Donnelly, in memoriam.)

Despite the archaeologists, no less
The anthropologists, let us respect
In hindsight that *he* was not visionless!
Let us approach in manner circumspect
His Pan-Atlantis Concept and Effect,
Adroitly correlating east and west:
Where factoid, fact, and fiction intersect,
An elder empire has he thus expressed,
From Egypt's riverbank to the western Islands of the Blest.

From Egypt's pyramids to those of Yucatán,
This elder empire still seems more than manifest,
And from Tenochtitlán to Teotihuacán.

To peer amid this terraced pyramid, alive with stone-carved imagery,
It makes a moment of apocalypse, a moment of sheer witchery.

Thursday morning, 10 November 2016.

The Nonsense Eater

Quark Ashcan Smiff

Sit down! I am the Inspector General!
I come to check your passports and your visas!
You shall fill out these forms (these endless forms).

(I'll do whatever nonsense you command—
I'll eat whatever nonsense you may spew—
I'm just a lowly guest or visitor.)

What do they do with all that information?
What hand I use with genitals and anus,
What toilet paper is it I prefer?
Am I retarded, or retired, or both;
Do I use a cane, or am I wheelchair-bound?
Can't they see? Can't they see that I need help?
Do I carry, or otherwise transport,
Suspect, or dangerous, material?—
Solid, liquid, inflammable, or bullets,
Gunpowder, pistols, rifles, daggers, knives, or swords,
Et cetera, et alia, et omnia!

Give me a break! I'm just a guest or tourist,
I've travelled halfway all around the planet,
To see your country's heralded attractions.
Give me a break! Why check my armpits, crotch,
Or anus? Have I drugs (or bombs) inside my body?
Or only legal medical prescriptions,
As packed amid my diverse toiletries?

Yes, let me in, and get me on my way
To see the remains, Ayutthaya, or Angkor,
Or whatever other ruins you may have;
The ancient ruins well preserved, the sole
Attraction without which no visitors would come
To meet your gracious people, mostly farmers,

Or people living in the access-towns,
All speaking their own local dialects.

Needless to say, should I have hostile thoughts,
Occasioned by these guards who do their job,
I keep them strictly to myself, no joking;
I will myself to seem amicable, and am.
Well, well, the guards at last, they wave me through.

So, get me to the nearest taxi-meter,
To take me to hotel, motel, or inn,
My hostelry with room and bath reserved,
Where I can drop my bags, and then pass out,
Prone on the bed, to sleep for several hours.

I have survived the trip, and passed through customs,
Their close inspection of my bags and body;
I kept my cool, and did not have a fit,
And I did not go crazy, or collapse.
In my mind's eye, I see, I still perceive,
Fiendish and grinning, the Inspector General,
And all the guards with their daemonic smiles.

I am ensconced in Southeast Asia, and within Thailand:
Please let me sleep, and dream of tropic islands.

So, all that checking, did it help, or was it nonsense?
At least no plane has blown up in mid-flight.

(Apologies and acknowledgments to G. Sutton Breiding for the title and for the pseudonym employed for Clark Ashton Smith.)

Between 10 and 15 November 2016

A King out of Macedonia

Alexander the Great! His name alone
Still resonates across the void of years,
A greater myth than any fabled throne.
Kind-hearted conqueror from alien spheres,
He laid to rest the conquered people's fears,
As he expanded his dominium:
His men became Hellenic pioneers.
He sought the oracle, the oraculum,
Inside Amoun's oasis temple at Ammonium.

Anointed as a son of Zeus by Siwah's priestly seers,
His freeing of the conquered folk led to delirium,
Confirmed him as a greater peer above his greatest peers.

Still singing out like trumpets, like a palace-burning flame,
Alexándros Megálos! What a name, and what a fame!

Tuesday morning, 15 November 2016.

Alexandros Megalos

His soldiers would have followed him to Hell
And back, so great the love they had for him,
And he for them: such bonds does need compel!
So beautiful of feature and of limb,
His face was like a light, the antonym
Of ugliness—his love, the utmost meed.
So strong a warrior, and yet not grim,
His mouth was like a wine of purest mead—
He might have figured on Olympus as another Ganymede.

He did not have one soldier who would not become his lover—
If he had even had the chance—who would not have agreed
To have become his lover-lad as well as any other.

Unique, he wore no beard, not only not to seem uncouth,
But just to bear the similitude of everlasting youth.

Tuesday afternoon, 15 November 2016.

Fountains

The fountains of the heavy winter rain,
Of the vertumnal, or the vernal, melted snow,
Wax more than equal to maintain
The levels where the deep-sea fountains flow,
Where currents fluctuate, and go
From any compass point, swing back and forth,
By solstice or by aequinox, thus in an endless throe,
To east or west, to south or north,
Encountering new realms like that dimension termed the fourth.

What greater miracle than to meet with some verdant lawn,
To lay the head upon some verdant sward, some verdant swarth,
Impromptu bed graced by some nymph and by her satyr-faun!

So let the fountains of the deep sea flow, to overwhelm our little place,
The struggle lies between the flush and go, always inside that interspace.

Tuesday evening, 15 November 2016.

Katnyptian

Sometime after I had turned five or six,
And already I had learned to read at school,
A book for me became the utmost fix:
Divine fixation that would henceforth rule
My life while I became an older fool—
Grandmother Fryer used a novel word:
I mused, but did not wish to seem uncool,
Before I asked her what she had averred,
My guess of what I thought I heard, or overheard:

She had warned someone to avoid some type "Katnyptian fit"—
Katnyptian, like Egyptian, what?—was that the sound I heard?
This *Katnypt,* like *Egypt?* what place was that, and where was it?

I boldly asked my question. Then she laughed as she explained.
The root was *catnip.* Yes, no Egypt anywhere contained.

Saturn-day morning, 19 November 2016.

A Song in Reverse

(An experiment.)

O aura fit for him that would have Death's embrace!
A dark perfume . . . of pure and perfect grace. . . .
Your face wherefrom pours forth perfume,
Upon your stem, your foliage, and your face—
Its utter black, its utter gloom,
As from some vast unlightened tomb,
Abyssal night bestows:
How much too darkly do you bloom,
O ebon-colored rose!

Between 9 and 28 November
2016: probably the 22nd.

A Sunday Noontide Ritual

Every Sunday we would visit my mother's parents,
Jean Teillière and Clarice Teillière, but born Dufresne,
Our Francophone grandfolks, thus the maternal side:
Of all our relatives, the closest and the best,
The most affectionate with kisses and with hugs,
Not grandmother, nor grandfather, but Mémère and Pépère,
Who had my brother and myself pronounce our first French words,
Thus Mémère and Pépère, for us to address them.

We ate a noontide feast prepared by chère Mémère;
Then after eats they would enact a curious ritual,
Which always frightened me, and otherwise amazed.
To the east of the table in the dining room,
Within the window bay two special armchairs stood,
Two leather rocking chairs that faced each other square,
With due space between them, a space that was discreet.

After each had sat down, they would begin to talk
About what had occurred, that is, the week just past.
A disagreement might sometimes come up by chance,
And this would often lead into a shouting match,
This acting as a safety valve for each of them.
They then would reconcile, and calmly quiet down,
Each one retiring to their separate bedchambers,
To have a nap, a Sunday hour or two of sleep.

While Uncle Roland had gone off in his convertible,
Pretty spiffy, and pretty grand, his pride and joy,
The rest of us—mother and sons—we also napped.
Often we would all sleep in uncle's own bedchamber,

Or Ronald my brother and I would each take turns
Resting with the one or the other of our grandfolks,
Feeling an extra warmth and love within the arc
Of a much older arm, as we lay side by side.

Between 19 and 28 November
2016; the 26th, probably.

Mouse in Boots

What if the mice assumed authority
By some odd act or alchemy of power,
Or by some author's own auctority?—
When, à la knighthood, mousehood was in flower,
When mice became the critters of the hour,
Then sacred to Apollo, god of light.—
When little critters had less need to cower,
When from the sacred Muses, no less bright,
They found a waiting refuge, and protection overnight.

And where was that? To wit, in any old or new Museum,
Where they could serve as little guards in boots throughout the night,
Better than what they could at any newsstand or news-eum!

Need forces them to shun the brighter light, the common day;
As for the bigger entities, to keep them faraway.

Monday morning, 28 November 2016.

The "X"—The Unknown Quantity

Of all the symbols man has used or made,
The X—the unknown quantity—alone
Puts all the other symbols in the shade.
Somehow to *qualify* what is *un*known
Is greater than to deal with what *is* known?—
To do so with an X: miraculous.
Somehow to *quantify* what is unknown
Is fabulous, if not fantabulous—
Through mathematics it still seems yet more miraculous!

In theory and in practise, what is said, or what is done,
Does not always agree, but rather is anomalous—
Despite disclaimers, there *is* something new beneath the sun.

That such is true, this business of the unknown X makes clear.
Item: Appearances are sometimes not what they appear.

Wednesday morning, 7 December 2016.

By the Light of Flambeaux

The torch-lit treasures in those treasure-caves
Gave off—among the stuff piled everywhere—
The fiery gleam of pure flame-gold in waves.
At once the scientists became aware
Of how much time it took, and love, and care,
For artists to make art from much of it.
Objects of use, of skill, piled everywhere—
Cups, statues, images, in most of it—
And in yet further caves, the prize in all of it!

Those ingots and ingots of orichalch, of pure flame-gold:
Earthquakes had left some order, no, in almost none of it,
Piled everywhere in any mode, as in a tale twice-told.

To list, to register, to catalogue, to classify,
A long time of travail to make some kind of sense of it:
Little escapes the sciences and their relentless eye.

Thursday morning, 15 December 2016.

The Grove of Ceiba Trees along the Stream

    Along the river but below the bound
    On which the compound stands within its wall,
    Some giant ceiba trees yet hold their ground.
    Where rainy-season high flood waters brawl,
    Where ceiba roots, enormous, writhe and sprawl,
    Deployed inside the basin of the stream—
    The winter shadows drop their soft sweet pall:
    Here nature and here beauty meet and scheme
    For giant ceiba trees to dream forevermore in dream.

    Even the tattered plastic bags, dispersed along the shore,
    Do not disturb unduly, nor the glamour nor the gleam,
    Nor yet the landscape's loveliness, as rooted at its core.

    Six feet above the river's bed, there at its lowest flow,
    The grove of ceiba trees appears forevermore to grow.

Winter Solstice,
Wednesday morning,
21 December 2016.

Those Giant Ceiba Trees Again

Why are the old big trees called patriarchs?—
Given the female principle of birth—
Are they not better termed as matriarchs?
How deep the ceiba trees descend in earth,
How buttressed the trunk, and how thick the girth,
One with the river and the riverside—
They grasp enough to sense, for what it's worth,
Not to compete, not to have even tried,
Among themselves, the ceiba trees, in splendor and in pride.

Only the local farmers grasp how this locale to con:
With little water in the stream, there is none for the tide,
Only the thin small trickle that flows from much higher on.

The cosmos has gone through a lot of trouble to exist,
And motivates its entities that they, too, should persist.

Thursday morning, 29 December 2016.

From Script to Script, From Crypt to Crypt

We go from one script to another script,
We con the stories and the documents.
We disinter the buried monuments,
Ambling from one crypt to another crypt.
The past holds all of us, all things, hard-gripped:
Our findings constitute the emoluments,
And for our thoughts increase the integuments,
Howevermuch we stay perforce tight-lipped.

But that is not the half of it, the moiety—
So, what then is revealed by archaeology,
If not the source of things, their etymology?
So, what comes therefore from historiography,
From legend, myth, and folklore, but the poetry,
The miracle, the madness, and the goety?

Friday morning, 6 January 2017.

On Jesse Allen's Biggest African Tableau

(La casa con el mural.)

The panorama-mural, the main house,
Hacienda Jalenco, Cesario Cristalinas,
Canton Zacamil, Candelaria de la Frontera,
El Salvador, December 2016-January 2017.

Since he himself has hymned with artful word
The passage of the elephants at night
Across the desert, moving as a herd:
Leconte de Lisle might take a real delight—
Thus going from the big cat on the right
Up to the elephants far to the left—
In this wide view, these colors fused with light,
Made real by brush strokes lavish, quick, and deft,
Inside this painted tapestry, its wondrous warp and weft.

Saturn-day afternoon, 7 January 2017.

"The Girl with the Ice Cream Tits"

(For Charlie Mountain, the artist who made
the original woodblock of the same name)

Voluptuous, abundant, beautiful,
This damozel has everything required—
The artist making her was dutiful
To chart each luscious curve, if not inspired
To have her go escorted, nay, esquired,
On out into the world, but with her band
Of stalwart fans, mixed up, enmeshed, and mired—
To which I, too, belong (if humble), and
With such impassioned lover-fans I needs must take my stand.

In truth she is a perfect Ice Cream Sundae of a girl:
Such sundry charms as hers, who could resist, who could withstand?
Well worthy she is of a tryst, a tumble, and a whirl!

Let us go seek together then, in some fold of the sky,
The Ice Cream Sundae Paradise, where-never found on high.

Monday morning, 9 January 2017.

The New Conquistadors

Now soon, as you yourself presage, the knights of Earth shall wend
Upon their quest, their destined quest, with all the stars for crown,
Into the hypercosmic Vast sublime and without end.
—D. Sidney-Fryer, "Kilcolman Castle."

Against the wall it hangs, a huge heraldic shield:
On the left side, a mounted armored knight; below,
A caravelle advancing west fills out the coign.
On the right side, space-accoutered the Space Man stands,
So bundled up he does look like Michelin Man.
Below, a spheroid space-craft with antennas out,
A Space Age galleon that sails on cosmic seas—
The technologic marvel that the ship remains,
Upon that sable ocean, thus the Vast, that Ocean Sea of space.

The new Conquistadors of Conquest or of Quest—
Conquest of Space? A striking phrase, but really Conquest?
So far, we have but edged a little from the shore.

A little humbleness would serve these human beings well.
So far, they have but made a mess of things, with worse to come.

Sunday morning, 15 January 2018.

Lo Ordinario

Ordinary words, ordinary phrases,
ordinary people, ordinary situations,
it all adds up to something
ordinary, ordinary, ordinary, ordinary.

We cannot live without
the ordinary, the everyday, the commonplace,
It occupies us, it employs us,
it feeds us, it preoccupies us,
and with good or very good reason.
We cannot live without it, period.

Yet we need imagination, and we need it
to do the most ordinary things.

But the heart, the soul, the imagination,
how seldom do they yearn after the ordinary,
but (rather) the vivid and the exotic,
the unknown and the many colored,
and not the grim and frightful:
imagination seeks imagination,
and its highest fruit,
the free play that is fantasy.

Tuesday morning, 17 January 2017.

A Maya Pyramid Revisited

When once upon a time, a long time since,
The Maya seemed the children of the skies,
They left us major works and subtle hints.
Would they have stopped in wonder, to surmise
How this place might appeal to future eyes,
Evoking vistas otherwise unknown?
Evoking shapes of monstrous form and size,
Herewith did priest-blown conches once intone
Their raucous fanfares to call people to this templed zone?

Look at these images up close: they might evoke some fear,
They might evoke some dread, an awe deep in our blood and bone—
These are the demons of this place, their genius loci here.

Do gods or demons linger there, where they have had a shrine?
Do these await awakening, what symbol, or what sign?

Sunday morning, 22 January 2017.

The Cup from Otherwhere

The cup, they said, was made of silver plate,
Inlayed with tiny gems of no great price—
However, the effect seemed profligate.
Its X-shaped, foot-high profile, in a trice
Revealed (apart from size) no strange device,
But that it could hold much inside its bowl.
Wine or whatever, what could then entice
Someone to pour yet more inside that hole
Beyond its daytime or its nighttime gain, decrease, or dole?

It had remained a dazzlement of rare design
That lured the drinkers to indulge beyond control,
Then set a limit not to oyerstep that line.

Intoxication in one sense does not know rule or bound,
Except those further depths to plumb, that further gulf to sound.

Sunday afternoon, 29 January 2017.

Divertissement

I

Where sylph and sylphide glide above the grass,
The moon-white glade is lightly tinged with blue;
Where they divert with village youth and lass,
They all partake of transcendental brew;
Where *faeries* and humans rendezvous,
Those otherworldly creatures con them well,
For whose divertissement they sport and woo,
With great good fun.—From just which coign or cell
Or sphere or country do they hail?—I cannot vouch or tell.

What did that *faerie* brew, that transcendental booze, contain?
A bit of moonshine's own, some amaranth, some asphodel?
Brewed from fermented grape, fermented hops, fermented grain?

It is a huge relief to know, for village youth and lass,
That somewhere still, the sylph, the sylphide, glide above the grass.

Wednesday evening, 8 February 2017.

Divertissement

II

Whatever sprite or imp might be involved,
Sylphide, sylph, dryad, naiad, oread,
That is, wood nymphs, water nymphs, mountain nymphs,
Elves, dwarves, fauns, satyrs, giant bats,
Goblins, poltergeists, kobolds, and nereids,
Howevermuch deployed in some fantastic narrative,
Laid out in so many acts, in so many tableaux,
As aptly realized upon the stage,
Displayed through drama, dance, and mime,
Embodied by means of the living flesh and blood and bones
Of dancer-actors-actresses—how fleet and strong!—
All this unfurls before our very eyes,
Enchanted vision utterly contrived,
An interlude and more of purposed make-believe.

Odd paradox that, inasmuch as the female star,
The prima ballerina, who seems so light,
So very much ethereal and otherworldly,
Is in truth as powerful as any sumo wrestler—
Beware the hidden strength within her legs,
Which skillfully directed and exploited
Could kill or maim or cripple!
Exquisite paradox that something otherworldly
Is only realized, that is, can only be made real,
Upon the stage, with sets and costumes, and with solid props,
With lovely tunes and melodies
Embodied forth in luscious orchestrations,
With piquancy, with pointed harmonies,
As played-performed by trained musicians,
Directed by some veteran conductor,
Who knows this kind of music very well,
And how to set it forth
In such a mode as to enchant

The audience that waits and wishes for enchantment.
The houselights dim, a rosy glow ensues,
The conductor comes in from the right
On into the orchestra pit
Where a full-fledged ensemble waits
The conductor's magic signal to begin,
As of when he lifts up his baton,
His fiddler's bow transformed.

Sunday morning, 12 February 2017.

Transition

As if of bronze or brass or copper hewn,
The leaves began to fade, but did not fall,
All on that perfect autumn afternoon.
The dazzling swirl of colors overall,
The feel and mood of autumn, of the fall,
How different from the vital burst of spring!
As the year's dusk yields to the winter's caul,
Where once the forest with bird-song would ring,
Now just the birds that migrate south: some honk, they do not sing.

Geese, herons, trumpeter and tundra swans, with whooping cranes—
Unparalleled sonorities they make while on the wing—
They seek those far, exotic shores where summer rules and reigns:

Are they en route to Otherwhere, so strong and swift they soar,
On towards another world, by cryptic gate, through cosmic door?

Sunday morning, 18 February 2017.

To H. P. L.—A Tribute out of Time

> "At best the cosmos is indifferent to humankind."
> —D. Sidney-Fryer, "Almost As If."

A genius writer, he was not above craft,
The endless care, to hammer out a tale,
This gentleman, this Howard Phillips Lovecraft.
And it was he who first showed me the trail
Into a world of wonder without fail,
However strange, however frightening.
To tell his cosmic truth, he did not quail,
But spoke with style, as if with lightening,
With dread and angst around the heart forever tightening.

"The Terrible Old Man"—could that not be Lovecraft himself?
Whatever test he might have set, it proves enlightening:
Do not lift that forbidden volume down from off that shelf!

Do not invoke those Ancient Ones for philtre, curse, or spell—
    Beware "The Shadow out of Time," and "The Colour out of Space."
Those existential parables have taught us more than well—
    To keep to where and what you know, to your own time and place.

(The Elder Gods, the Ancient Ones: theocracy, anyone?)

Sunday morning, 5 March 2017.

A Bit of Nostalgia

(Sacramento, the state capital, receives in honor the
Queen of England, 5 March 1983, 11 A.M. to 3 P.M.)

Elizabeth the Second came to town,
To Sacto-Town, with Philip, Consort Prince:
She dressed in green, but did not wear a crown.
An Old West and a history fan long since,
She visited, first, Sutter's Fort, and thence
The Capitol, refurbished and rebuilt:
And all restored with gilded monuments—
That splendor would not early fade or wilt—
Because of storage time, the statues well deserved their gilt.

The Queen enjoyed it all, but in especial Sutter's Fort—
That hour-long visit at that site—she loved it to the hilt,
As rangers guided her, and paid her unobtrusive court.

The luncheon in the Capitol? It turned out pretty fair.
Once more the motorcade, but back to the aëroport
The Queen and Consort vanished quite, far up into the air.

Sunday morning, 12 March 2017.

The Hunting of the Ampersand

> The country mouse and the city mouse
> were having a lively chat:
> The country mouse was tall and thin,
> the other short and fat.
> —From an Old Rime by "Anonymouse."

[The three blind mice had had their interview
From that kind social-worker-bureaucrat
Who reassured them of their legal due:
A full immunity from dog or cat,
Perhaps adoption by a plutocrat—
Dark glasses with tin cup and small white cane:
And when their spirits drooped completely flat,
Or when they might feel agony or pain,
They could receive a sniff or two of quality cocaine.]

(Item: Some social work updated for our rodent friends.)

The one stood not so tall, the other not so fat,
More agreeably plump, or rather, amply fleshed;
The country or the farmer mouse was thin and spare.
His rodent peers called him the Count, or simply Count;
The Duke, or simply Duke, the city mouse was named.
As for their mutual friend, the church or temple mouse,
He could not meet them at that time, but would another day.
They called this friend, the church mouse, Rev, or Reverend,
But if he sermonized, he kept it brief, and to the point.

They shared a common problem they could not escape,
That they had named the haunting by the Ampersand,
Which only happened when they tried to sleep at night.
This monster haunted them but only in their dreams,
But that was bad enough when most they needed rest.
It always happened on the same night for all three,
For all of them, a nightmare and a monster-beast,
And christened by the church mouse as the Ampersand:
It certainly disturbed the even tenor of their days.

The even tenor of their life, such as it was:
The country or the farmer mouse lived in a barn,
And in a safe and little hole inside a beam;
Not fancy, but cozy, it suited him just fine.
The city mouse? He occupied a fancy loft—
No dogs or cats—and where the live-in family
Not only tolerated him, but welcomed him,
And treated him as what he had become, a pet:
No dog or cat could have enjoyed a better life.

As for their prudent friend, the church or temple mouse,
He did not live inside the church, but in the rectory,
Inside a hole within the wall, concealed with art.
Yes, with a little painting that portrayed a mouse!
What was it country mouse and city mouse discussed,
What did they talk about so animatedly?
Their friend, the temple mouse, had had a bright idea,
Which he proceeded to propose to his two friends,
The Ampersand? Just what could be this Ampersand?

A fanciful chimaera, or a figment of the mind?
A mere illusion, some imaginary beast?
A bugaboo spawned by fatigue, by lack of sleep?
Authentic monster-beast? A reject from the brain?
A cast-off of the many mirrors in the head?
A cast-off of the coiling lobes inside the skull?
Or could it be a phantom crittur from the veldt?
How might the three mice then escape the haunting by this beast?

They must go hunt this Ampersand, to seek him out,
Wherever he might live, wherever he might lair,
To kill or capture him, so they might sleep once more,
Thus undisturbed by nightmare or by ghastly dream.
The three mice had conjoined in solemn consultation
At midnight to decide how they should now proceed—
In what locale, perhaps remote, or near at hand,
In desert wilderness, in jungled labyrinth,
A nightmare beast, in proper nightmare countryside.

A nightmare countryside they wanted to avoid,
A nightmare quest they wanted to avoid as well,
Especially a Werner Herzog nightmare quest:
They all had thought of that with dread, but Duke it was
Who said out loud, point-blank, what they did not desire:
No Sahara, no Amazon, no Central Africa,
No Gobi waste, no burning sands unlimited.
But it might end up that they had no choice at all;
They would need to go where their quest would lead them on.

They had no clue. Should they consult a fortune-teller,
An humble fortune-teller, or some higher guide?
Some noted mystic, but with thaumaturgic powers,
With recognized certificate, with recognized credentials,
Known far and wide, both north and south, both east and west?
Where could a guide like that be found? In the Far East?
Or it might be, in the Far West, of the U.S.—?
Who could this wise man be, this recluse, this guru?
All at once the church mouse blurted out, "Kerchieff!"

The other mice repeated after him, "Kerchieff?"
The Rev, "Yes, Ivan Ivanovich Kerchieff!
I hear that he resides middling high on Mount Shasta:
Let us go seek him out for his advice and help!
I know that, like Apollo, he is fond of mice.
That is us! We are mice! Let us prepare to visit him.
Let us prepare our little kits, our old backpacks,
The mouse-kits that we wore as little kids, remember?
We called ourselves the Three or Triple Mouse-kit-teers!"

The three mice lived in and around the capital,
The capital of California, Sacramento.
They somehow had to get from there up to Mount Shasta,
And made their practical arrangements for the nonce.
With mouse-kits on their backs they hitch-hiked up to Shasta:
Who could resist the Three or Triple Mouse-kit-teers—
The darnedest cutest varmints who had ever lived?
Arriving there, they climbed forthwith, and found the cave
Where abode Ivan Ivanovich Kerchieff.

They found themselves amazed by his mode of existence!
Far from relaxing on a bed of nails or glass,
He had his home inside a lavish palace-cave
Tapestried and floored with expensive Persian carpets—
Such as he had sold once to Hollywoodland stars.
After they bowed, and introduced themselves to him,
The three mice made note of his water pipe and samovar.
He smiled at them down from his lotus-like position:
"Be welcome, be assured, I recognize why you have come."

At first amazed, they passed to sheer astonishment:
He smiled again, and offered them some tchai, some tea.
As they all sat imbibing from their little cups,
He spoke, "You can locate, confront, and quash this beast,
This Ampersand, as you have named him heretofore,
But only in Death Valley, at some real risk to yourselves.
Beyond this datum, I can give you no advice—
You must decide among yourselves what you must do!"
Somewhat chagrined, they nodded, and gave him their thanks.

When he had said Death Valley, how their hearts had sunk!
Later some food would come, and they could sleep there for the night.
The next day, after breakfast, as they leave, he speaks,
"You must make do without my further sage advice,
Every man, every mouse, becomes his own guru,
But you will do alright among the three of you;
Goodbye, good luck, take heart!" They bowed, and spoke their thanks.
Proceeding down the mountainside, they hitch-hiked home:
After due rest the great adventure loomed ahead.

En route hitch-hiking home, they scarcely said a word
But once they rested for the night, and ate their morning meal,
Duke blurted out, "Death Valley! That's impossible,
It is in fact enormous, north and south, and wide!—
Unless we start midmost, and at the town itself,
If that is what he meant, but he said nothing more.
The great guru vouchsafed us what? A mystery,
Another mystery! Why bother to have asked?"
The other mice assented, nodding back at Duke.

They sat at home within the farmer mouse's barn,
When suddenly a big bird landed in their midst
With scroll tied to his leg. He clawed it off, and gave
It in his beak to Duke, who opened it at once.
"Look, it's from Kerchieff! Please note, it's new advice,
That Mono Lake might make the best locale of all
To find and quash the Ampersand." What should they do?
A much less challenging locale, they sighed with great relief:
They all consented to subscribe to this big change in plans.

The Reverend pulled out a map that he unfurled.
"Here's Mono Lake, east of Yosemite, on through Tioga Pass,
At thirty-eight degrees of latitude, no less
Than at one hundred nineteen grades of longitude.
I know the place, it has an island one square mile
Not quite dead center in the middle of the lake.
If Mono is the place, that's where our beast would live,
Would have his lair, right there inside that island's bound,
At that conjunction point of longitude and latitude."

His fellow mice, his rodent peers, looked hard at him,
The Reverend, in wonder and astonishment.
They both spoke up at once, and both at the same time:
"You're right! That's it! It must be it! It has to be!
I'll be a mouser's uncle, if that is not it!
You're a marvel, Rev, you really are a marvel!"
The Reverend? He smiled, nodding in satisfaction,
"I'm glad you both concur. It *is* worth the attempt.
Let us all sleep on it, and start off in the morning."

Well rested and refreshed, with their backpacks refilled,
Our Three or Triple Mousekitteers, all cute as buttons,
Departed from the barn, just west of Sacramento,
And hitch-hiked easily to Stockton and Manteca,
No incident or accident to bar the way,
And switched from Highway Ninety-nine on over to One Twenty,
Thus veering at Manteca thus from south to east,
Passing through Oakdale, Chinese Camp, as well as Groveland,
South of Hetch-Hetchy Reservoir, to Tuolumne Meadows.

They left the valley floor, passed through the wooded foothills,
And on into the wooded mountains rising on all sides,
The springtime beauty everywhere in truth breathtaking.
They passed on through Tioga Pass, descending to the townlet,
The village, of Lee Vining on its western shore.
There Mono Lake spread out within its wider basin,
There stood the Mono Craters, to the south of the lake,
And there four miles or so offshore, to the northeast,
There lay the one square mile, the white isle of Paoha.

Here where the lake extends along the state's east edge,
Here to the east of the Sierra Nevada range,
Almost directly next to the border with Nevada,
This was old Paiute Indian land, the Indians mostly gone.
Our Triple Mousekitteers? They stood there on the shore,
Somewhat intimidated by the desolation,
Looking out over to the terrain of their goal,
The place where they aspired to finish up their quest,
To find, confront, and quash the dreaded Ampersand.

Impressing them like all the other visitors,
Rising up offshore stood a grove of tufa towers,
The so-called tufa towers, but other words could work as well:
Stalagmites, turrets, posts, but there is no *mot juste*.
The country mouse, he sighed and said, "All very well and good,
But these piles cannot help or hinder this our quest:
We must find a way to the island, and then back.
Any ideas, anyone?" He smiled before continuing,
"Let us wait until tomorrow, we have had a long day."

Duke and Rev consented; so the three pitched their camp
In an evergreen grove not so far from the shore:
The little town had many trees distributed throughout.
Unless disturbed by dogs or cats, they should sleep well enough.
After their meal they got inside their sleeping bags;
And soundly slept all night without untoward incident.
They woke up with the sun, consumed their little meal,
And went back to the shore, where they stood for a while:
They had to figure out how they would reach the island.

Paoha it was called, the place of water sprites,
And rumored to be dangerous, or could they be
Another mere projection of the Ampersand?—
And never mind the sudden storms that could come up!
Meanwhile they had to solve how they would reach the island.
The country mouse was quietly exploring by the shore,
Among some rushes, when he said, "Look what I found!"
The others hurried over to the spot, and looked:
Some child had left a toy rowboat with oars intact!

The mice bailed out a little liquid in the hull,
And pulled the boat a little out into the water,
Where they got in the vessel, the church mouse at the oars.
They now took turns while rowing on towards the island—
They had reached it sometime around the middle of the morning.
They went ashore to find the spot to meet the beast,
Which they sensed would take place but inland at high noon.
Going inland, they found a glade, an open level space,
And all agreed, "This is the spot where he shall show."

"Let us rest here, and save our strength, until he shows."
And thus they waited patiently until high noon.
A little bit before that time an older man
Entered the glade, and noted them all in attendance.
Speaking the ancient tongue common to man and beast,
He asked them what or whom it was they were awaiting.
Trusting his confidence, they patiently explained
Their nightmare-pestered sleep: the old man understood,
And asked, "Were any of the monsters anything like this?"

He stood midmost the glade as veils and shades appeared,
And wrapped him all around—he almost disappeared
Inside a whirlwind swirl out of which then emerged
A dragon-shape, immense, whose hot and heavy breath
Breathed out upon the mice, and frightened them to death,
Or almost so—they held their breath, and scarcely dared to breathe.
The dragon changed at once into a giant spider,
Of such a size as to defy our planet's gravity,
Who then advanced upon our mice—they closed their eyes.

They opened them again, and what was it they saw?
A lovely giantess groomed and gowned gorgeously,
And of such beauty as to take away their breath.
She came up close, and with one finger stroked each one,
So unexpectedly it almost caused them fear.
A flash of light, the shape had changed yet once again—
In her stead stood a youth of otherworldly beauty:
He spoke, "I am Apollo, in a sense your god and father
It is myself who acted as the Ampersand."

The Triple Mousekitteers in awe looked at each other,
All while their father-god continued holding forth:
"I put you to the test, to prove once and for all,
That mice can act as brave as anyone of old,
That mice, too often thought as mild or timid creatures,
Are only wise and cautious, given their small size,
But they can be as brave as any fabled heroes."
Supremely beautiful, the Muses then appeared,
To dance around their father-god, an act of homage.

Waking up as though from a long-since former life,
Somehow the three mice find themselves back in the barn,
As if they had awakened from a nightmare-dream.
So, after all, was it then but a nightmare or a dream?
As the three mice discussed the topic, all at once
Apollo in a flash of light—supreme illumination—
Appeared, and smiled, and spoke, "Yes, it was all quite real."
He vanished, and the mice regarded each among themselves
In marvel and surmise. Would wonders never cease?

Wednesday, 15 March 2017—
Thursday, 30 March 2017.

Notes

by Dlanod Yendis

St. Ichabod.
The *Guinness Book of Records* in the later 1900s reported a domestic cat in England, Himmy, at 39 pounds.

Swimming Somewhere in the Antillias.
The site specified in this poem, that is, in Greater (or Greatermost) Antillia would locate somewhere along the extensive southern shore of Cuba that runs east and west not quite 200 miles.

A Colonnade out of Time.
This remnant of a mainland Atlantean colony east of Atkantharia would sit somewhere east of the Canary Islands in southern Morocco, thus in extreme northwestern Africa.

Where Now the Towns of Legend and of Myth?
Tatu, also given as Day-du or Daidu.
Relevant dates for Kubla Khan, 1215-1294. China's Great Khan, 1260-1294. Proclaims himself Emperor of China in 1279.

And Have You Seen a Peacock as of Late?
When the peacock's tail spreads out on into the gigantic fan, its overall area seems around twenty-six times the bird's body-image-silhouette. Somehow getting loose, the peacock limned in this poem had wandered off out of some neighbor's property, gracing other homesteads with his presence, including that one serving at that time as home for the author-poet. Thanks to some other benevolent neighbors, the bird eventually made it back to his home turf, miraculously uninjured by vehicular traffic along a fairly busy country road. (Queue, here: anus.)

Retrospective.
Ind or Ynd is an older (poetic) term for India or the Indies, pronounced with both a short i and a long i.

Enigma.
This Roman villa would sit somewhere along the Sorrento coast south of Naples and east of Capri, that is, according to the evidence in the poem itself.

The Transcendence of King Bhumibol.
    Born in 1928, Bhumibol Adulyadej died on 13 October 2016.
    Reigning for seventy years, he died at eighty-eight. Among much else of a musical nature he composed the current national anthem, and aficionados consider him an exceptional musician, as well as a fine jazz performer-improvisor. He came to the throne after the mysterious death of his elder brother, the king Ananda Mahidol, on 9 July 1946 in the old Grand Palace.

Another Forsaken Garden.
The Forsaken Garden Again.
    Both titles refer to "A Forsaken Garden" in the Second Series of the *Poems and Ballads* by A. C. Swinburne. The estate limned in these two poems (evidently still extant) would lie somewhere between Narragansett Bay, Rhode Island, and Buzzard's Bay, enclosed in southeastern Massachusetts.

Artorius, Arthurius, or Arthur Rex?
    Geoffrey Ashe recently identified (in the latter 1900s, and thus in the wake of Castle Cadbury-Camelot) "Dux Bellorum" Arthur as that prince or king R(h)iothamus of Britanny and possibly of Great Britain. However, Leslie Alcock, as the most eminent Arthurian-period archaeologist, has not confirmed this identification.

The Lyre-Bird.
    The three species of this unusual avian are all native to "Oz," that is, Australia.

On Jesse Allen's Biggest African Tableau.
    Leconte de Lisle celebrates the elephants moving across the nocturnal desert in the haunting lyric with epic overtones, *Les Éléphants.*

Upon a Maya Pyramid in El Salvadore.
    American lawyer, politician, reformer, etc. (and also something of a poet in speculative prose), Ignatius Donnelly (1831–1901) propounded many fascinating theories with his various books whether factual or fictional. His titles include *Atlantis: The Antediluvian World* (1882), his first and most popular monograph, followed by

another apocalyptic study, *Ragnarok* (1883).

His later titles include *The Great Cryptogram* (1888); *The Cipher in the Plays and on the Tombstone* (1889); and the novel *Caesar's Column* (1891). The second of these titles claims to have found a cipher, a key, in Shakespeare's plays and on the tombstone of Sir Francis Bacon, a key that reveals and proves that Bacon actually created Shakespeare's plays. This theory fostered the celebrated Bacon-Shakespeare controversy, which persists to this day.

Caesar's Column remains quite a noteworthy example of an avant-garde and prophetic science fiction novel, which predicted many later modern inventions (machines and appliances) that ultimately came into existence and common usage.

Disregarding on our part later archaeology, anthropology, and other modern sciences, Donnelly makes quite a convincing case (following Plato) for Atlantis as a plausible (and not overlarge) island continent in the (North) Atlantic Ocean, that is, somewhere north of the equator, as the seat of an empire including lesser island kingdoms, and as the center of a civilization that influenced quite a few peoples to the east (such as the Egyptians) and to the west (such as the Maya, the Toltecs, and the Aztecs).

A Bit of Nostalgia. (5 March 1983.)

The jet airplane carrying the Queen and her Consort actually touched down on the tarmac of the Sacto Metro Airport at 10:56 A.M. The Queen coincidentally was fifty-six at the time. The local newspaper alerted the poet-author to the thirty-fourth anniversary of the event; *The Sacramento Bee,* Sunday, 5 March 2017: *From the Archive;* "Queen's Quick City Tour—Fort, Capitol," article by Ronald W. Powell, a short exceptional piece distinguished by poetic suggestiveness.

And where was I, the poet-author?! A friend had alerted me to the route to be taken by the Queen's motorcade en route from the Fort to the Capitol. I had walked over to 25th and K from the house that I shared with two other friends on J near 25th, dressed in a tank top and gym shorts (I still have those clothes). Although forty-nine, I looked more like thirty-nine or younger, and I still looked like a hunk. I still had cute young gay guys whistle at me on the street! (Huh?)

The motorcade went past, the official limousine (with Queen, Consort, and Governor) hemmed in by other vehicles and by highway police before and aft. I caught a glimpse of Queen and Consort! They looked just like themselves! I was thrilled, and still am thrilled, after all those years! The Queen and her Consort would not have noticed me, but a few of the other people in the motorcade looked my way, and smiled. For me it remains an epiphany!

The Hunting of the Ampersand.
The big island called Paoha measures about two miles north and south, and about one mile east and west, probably closer to two square miles than the one square mile in the text of the poem. The island lies four miles or so northeast of Lee Vining, or where Lee Vining Creek debouches into Mono Lake. *Mono* here refers to the (alkali) fly, and *paoha* to some water spirits.

ABOUT THE POET

Poet, performing artist, critic, and literary historian, Donald Sidney-Fryer is the last in the great line of California Romantics that reaches from Ambrose Bierce to George Sterling, from Sterling to his protégé Clark Ashton Smith, and from Smith to his disciple Sidney-Fryer.

Carrying on the tradition of "pure poetry" begun in early modern English by Edmund Spenser and revivified by the English and American Romantic poets (Samuel Coleridge, William Wordsworth, John Keats, Percy Bysshe Shelley, Alfred, Lord Tennyson, and Edgar Allan Poe), long after the mainstream poetic establishment had abandoned it, the California Romantics created two monuments in verse, Sterling with *A Wine of Wizardry* and Smith with *The Hashish-Eater*.

During his long career Sidney-Fryer has given dramatic readings from these poets and from Edmund Spenser's epic *The Faerie Queene,* across the U.S. and Great Britain. He has written and edited over two dozen books and booklets. He has edited four books by Smith for Arkham House, and three paperbacks, also by Smith, for Pocket Books, in addition to *A Vision of Doom*, 50 of the best poems by Ambrose Bierce, published by Donald M. Grant, who has also brought out Sidney-Fryer's *Emperor of Dreams: A Clark Ashton Smith Bibliography*.

From 1980 to 1999 Sidney-Fryer assembled *The Case of the Light Fantastic Toe* (still awaiting publication), his historical monograph on the Romantic ballet. As a poet Sidney-Fryer has crafted *Songs and Sonnets Atlantean* (the first series), the final book to appear from Arkham House under the personal supervision of its founder August Derleth; as well as the Second Series, published by Wildside Press; and the Third Series, brought out by Phosphor Lantern Press; all these are subsumed into an omnibus edition.

Moreover, Sidney-Fryer has accomplished his chief prosodic innovation, the creation of the Spenserian stanza-sonnet, long before the recent and welcome emergence of the group of poets known as the New Formalists, who have restored a much needed and long overdue balance to the ongoing evolution of American poetry and poetics.

Although he resided in Southern California during 1998–2013, the self-styled Last of the Courtly Poets presently lives in Woodland, California.

www.ingramcontent.com/pod-product-compliance
Lightning Source LLC
Chambersburg PA
CBHW071003160426
43193CB00012B/1890